E. E. Jenkins

Sermons Delivered in the Wesleyan Chapel, Madras

Second Edition

E. E. Jenkins

Sermons Delivered in the Wesleyan Chapel, Madras
Second Edition

ISBN/EAN: 9783337160456

Printed in Europe, USA, Canada, Australia, Japan

Cover: Foto ©Lupo / pixelio.de

More available books at **www.hansebooks.com**

SERMONS

BY THE

REV. E. E. JENKINS, M.A.

SERMONS

DELIVERED IN THE WESLEYAN CHAPEL,
MADRAS.

BY

E. E. JENKINS, M.A.

WESLEYAN MISSIONARY.

Second Edition.

LONDON:
HAMILTON, ADAMS, & CO., PATERNOSTER ROW;
SOLD ALSO AT 66, PATERNOSTER ROW.
1866.

LONDON:
PRINTED BY HAYMAN BROTHERS,
GOUGH SQUARE, E.C.

CONTENTS.

SERMON I.

PHIL. iii. 13.—*This one thing I do* 1

SERMON II.

ISAIAH vi. 1—4.—*In the year that King Uzziah died I saw also the Lord sitting upon a throne, high and lifted up, and his train filled the temple. Above it stood the seraphims: each one had six wings; with twain he covered his face, and with twain he covered his feet, and with twain he did fly. And one cried unto another, and said, Holy, holy, holy, is the Lord of hosts: the whole earth is full of his glory. And the posts of the door moved at the voice of him that cried, and the house was filled with smoke* 16

SERMON III.

JOHN v. 17.—*My Father worketh hitherto, and I work* . 34

SERMON IV.

HOSEA ii. 21, 22.—*And it shall come to pass in that day, I will hear, saith the Lord, I will hear the heavens, and they shall hear the earth; and the earth shall hear the corn, and the wine, and the oil; and they shall hear Jezreel* 49

SERMON V.

EZEKIEL i. 1.—*Now it came to pass in the thirteenth year, in the fourth month, in the fifth day of the month, as I was among the captives by the river Chebar, that the heavens were opened, and I saw visions of God* . . 61

SERMON VI.

MATT. xxviii. 16—20.—*Then the eleven disciples went away into Galilee, into a mountain where Jesus had appointed them. And when they saw him, they worshipped him: but some doubted. And Jesus came and spake unto them, saying, All power is given unto me in heaven and in earth. Go ye therefore, and teach all nations, baptizing them in the name of the Father, and of the Son, and of the Holy Ghost: teaching them to observe all things whatsoever I have commanded you: and, lo, I am with you alway, even unto the end of the world. Amen* 77

SERMON VII.

ACTS xvi. 30.—*What must I do to be saved?* . . 93

SERMON VIII.

2 TIM. ii. 13.—*If we believe not, yet he abideth faithful: he cannot deny himself* 105

SERMON IX.

HEBREWS vii. 25.—*Wherefore he is able also to save them to the uttermost that come unto God by him, seeing he ever liveth to make intercession for them* . . . 118

SERMON X.

ZECH. ix. 17.—*How great is his goodness, and how great is his beauty!* 132

SERMON XI.

MAL. iv. 2.—*Unto you that fear my name shall the Sun of Righteousness arise with healing in his wings* . . 147

CONTENTS. vii

SERMON XII.

2 TIM. ii. 3.—*Endure hardness as a good soldier of Jesus Christ* 162

SERMON XIII.

1 PETER iii. 8.—*Be courteous* 177

SERMON XIV.

MATT. xv. 8.—*Their heart is far from me* 190

SERMON XV.

REV. iii. 14, 15, 16.—*And unto the angel of the church of the Laodiceans write: These things saith the Amen, the faithful and true witness, the beginning of the creation of God; I know thy works that thou art neither cold nor hot: I would thou wert cold or hot. So then because thou art lukewarm, and neither cold nor hot, I will spue thee out of my mouth* 202

SERMON XVI.

1 KINGS xix. 11, 12, 13.—*And he said, Go forth, and stand upon the mount before the Lord. And, behold, the Lord passed by, and a great and strong wind rent the mountains, and brake in pieces the rocks before the Lord; but the Lord was not in the wind: and after the wind an earthquake; but the Lord was not in the earthquake: and after the earthquake a fire; but the Lord was not in the fire: and after the fire a still small voice. And it was so, when Elijah heard it, that he wrapped his face in his mantle, and went out, and stood in the entering in of the cave* 218

SERMON XVII.

LUKE x. 42.—*But one thing is needful: and Mary hath chosen that good part, which shall not be taken away from her* . 235

CONTENTS.

SERMON XVIII.

GEN. v. 24.—*And Enoch walked with God : and he was not ; for God took him* 249

SERMON XIX.

GEN. v. 24.—*And Enoch walked with God : and he was not ; for God took him* 266

SERMON XX.

ISAIAH lxi. 3.—*Beauty for ashes* 281

SERMON I.

PHIL. iii. 13.

"This one thing I do."

THIS is the language of men who subdue the world,—the motto of all heroes, the secret of all triumph. A study of the sentiment that awakens words like these will enable us to account for those grand achievements in the history of mankind which are flattered into prodigies and miracles of genius. We can hardly imagine anything impossible to the man who says, "This one thing I do." We here observe one of those laws of compensation by which Nature would atone for the inequality of her gifts. All men have not great talents; but all men may have great industry; and as talents are useless without diligence, one talent improved by honest labour will make a greater man than ten that rust unused. But the cultivation of talents is only a means to an end. The man who educates his mind for great deeds and never attempts them, has about the same claim to distinction as a warrior who shows his skill on parade, but shuns fighting. *He* is the great man who sets before himself the attainment of an object worthy his powers, who has counted the cost of sacrifices, measured the impeding strength of difficulties, and bends his single soul to the task of winning. The mind, under this stimulus, is a glorious object: it can be but " a little lower than the angels ;" and is, unquestionably, the image of God. It is a sight worthy to attract a cloud of heavenly witnesses,—a mind sternly, yet serenely resolved to grasp a distant prize ; chilled by no hardship, disconcerted by no failure, exhausted by no delay, that gathers strength in its march like the shining light, makes stepping-stones of obstacles, auxiliaries of adversaries, and places all its inclinations under martial law, until victory be gained.

Such a mind, such a pursuit, and such a victory, had Paul, whose words we have taken as the basis of our address. It may be said of this eminent person that his entire life was an illustration of the text, *This one thing I do.* As a lad, he was bent upon scholarship, and won honors at the feet of Gamaliel: as a member of the Jewish church, he aspired to the very highest position that church could offer him ; and by his prodigal ability, his flaming zeal, and a consistency which no public character at that time could rival, he soon placed himself beyond parallel, and became the hope of a falling state: as a convert to Christianity, he was the same man in singleness and intensity of purpose; for in his capacity as a Christian, he resolved to scale the highest heaven of revelation and enjoyment permitted to mortals; in his calling as an Apostle he travelled more miles, endured more privations, established more churches, and filled a wider circuit of influence and popularity than all the other Apostles together. You will observe that the mind of this wonderful man dwelt mainly upon the unattained object: until that was within his grasp, he considered nothing gained: he availed himself of every personal help, he divested himself of every imaginary hinderance; his whole life was a fight, a race, a struggle, for the unattained, not for the *unattainable:* for with all the heat and enthusiasm of his temper, the habit of his mind was as practical and his judgment was as discreet, as that of the coolest utilitarian. "I so run, not uncertainly, so fight I, not as one that beateth the air." Paul was not understood by a selfish world: what great man is? We are not surprised that he was deemed a madman, the knight-errant of an impossible revolution.

What an admirable reference he makes to this estimate of his character, *Whether we be beside ourselves, it is to God: or whether we be sober, it is for your cause: for the love of Christ constraineth us.*

There is another feature in Paul's character that enforces the most important lesson we can derive from his history, and places him in instructive contrast with other enthusiasts. He arrogates to himself no particular saintship, no degree of holiness to which he does not invite others; his fellow disciples are not left to infer that his path is accessible to no traveller but himself, that they are not called to suffer and labour like him. He preaches to sinners as one who had been the chief of sinners; he preaches to Christians as a fellow-citizen with them of the household of God; he mingles with his brethren as one of the least of those who had received grace to preach the unsearchable riches of Christ. His letters abound with recognitions and exhortations implying that his converts were in fellowship with him; that the race and the fight were theirs no less than his; that his life did not stand out in exceptional proportions of faith, exertion, and fidelity, which the ordinary Christian was not expected to acquire and manifest. In all the egotism for which his character was remarkable he assumed nothing: it was the egotism of leadership, the self-assertion that cheers the depressed follower, and reassures the doubtful: for Paul himself, separate from his position, was remarkable for lowliness and modesty of self-estimation. His great individuality was the joint result of simplicity and ardour: he could not have been other than he was—a cedar of God's own rearing, the loftiest growth of Lebanon!

Now what was the one thing that Paul did? He pressed towards the mark for a prize: he designates it, *The prize of God's high calling;* the prize which God invites us to contend for, and which the successful candidate receives at the end of his course: "I have finished my course," said Paul, when in after years he was called to suffer for the truth, "henceforth there is laid up for me a crown of righteousness." To receive that crown from the Lord the righteous Judge, in the day of His appearing, was the single object of Paul's life. It is not my purpose to describe this prize itself, but Paul's manner of winning it. "Forgetting the things that are behind and reaching forth unto those things which are before, I press towards the mark," &c. It is impossible to do justice to language so animated and vigorous as this. You see before you a man agonizing to win a race. He is running with competitors for a prize. Everything that would trammel the motion of his body thrown away, he is simply arrayed in that which girds and braces him up for agility and endurance: he has measured the abilities of his rivals: he has carefully examined the race ground—its inequalities, its distance, and those exciting turns in the course which will strain his powers most, and indicate to spectators his chance of winning; he has anticipated the anguish of the last few steps, and the closing bound that proclaims his triumph or disgrace. His body has been thoroughly trained for the feat by a hard discipline of temperance and exercise. See this man, thus equipped and endowed, running to win the prize! his temper wrought up to the terrible calmness of a stedfast passion: that passion under the control of a wary discretion, and the whole man animated by a sure and certain hope. He does not waste his energy upon a single false step: he has no eye for a passing object, no recollection of an object passed: he looks straight before him, and as he leaps over the ground, he exults to see the prospect narrow and the goal draw near; his hope flies before him, claims the prize by anticipation, and like a good angel holds the glittering trophy steadily before his sight, and beckons him on; *he presses towards the mark,* he collects himself for the final struggle, the last steps; every muscle starts at the new strain, every nerve is maddened by a perilous tension; the entire frame is swayed to and fro under the tumult of its exertions; another leap, and shouts of crowding witnesses tell him the goal is past!

Such is the type by which the Holy Ghost instructed Paul to illustrate the course of the Christian, and this type found its fulfilment in Paul's life. There are always some minor points of difference between a type and its original: in the present instance the likeness between them is very striking, the parallel scarcely deviating all through the comparison. The most important matter for our consideration is the nature of Paul's progress—*Forgetting the things that are behind and reaching forth unto those things which are before.*

What are those things which Paul left behind and forgot?

1. He forgot whatever he had given up for Christ; as he says in the context, "What things were gain to me, those I counted loss for Christ." He forgot them in the sense of neglecting them. He had surrendered his

beloved Judaism, the pride of his family, the sphere of his personal ambition, the hope of his fortune: he had renounced his pharasaic righteousness—that solemn exactness of ceremonial obedience which was the stronghold of the Jew: he had forsaken his high family connexions, of which circle he had probably been the admiration and the joy: his friendships, his fellowships, his beloved rivalries, his schemes of advancement, all had gone; he had exchanged them for Christ and dishonour, Christ and poverty, Christ and the hatred of all, Christ and painful labour, Christ and a chain, a tribunal, and the prospect of a shameful death! and not only never repented these sacrifices, he forgot them, neglected to think of them, except to expose their vanity and worthlessness. I do count them but dung, said he, that I may win CHRIST. The Israelites fondly recollected the fleshpots of Egypt, and longed to resume their carnal plenty and base captivity. There are Christians also who find it hard to forget what they gave up for Christ, and dispute with themselves, whether in the sensitive jealousy of their first love, they did not make unnecessary sacrifices for their Master. The man who calculates with even a tincture of discontent what he has suffered for Jesus, has never seen the Cross!

It is impossible for those who have derived their ideas of duty from Him *who washed us from our sins in His own blood*, to refer with selfish misgiving to what they have done or left behind for Christ.

2. Paul forgot the error sand doubts that marked his first approaches to Christ.

He never said but once, *Who art thou, Lord?* He never said but once, *What wilt thou have me to do?* As soon as it pleased the Father to reveal His Son in the soul of Paul, and the feet of the new convert were fixed on the Rock of ages, he disentangled his mind for ever from the elements or rudiments that typified and foreshadowed Christ: having found Christ Himself, he broke away from the shadows, as a man who emerges from the gloom of a dungeon into broad day; and never returned to those "beggarly elements," as did some of his brethren. Have you never admired the clear and decisive style of Paul's experimental writings? Christ stands out from them evidently, as the sun in the heavens. Everything else is thrown into the back-ground, types, carnal ordinances, controversies, traditions, and the wisdom and philosophy of the world—their unsubstantial nature is laid bare, their luminous appearance is seen to be borrowed; the wandering eye is directed to Jesus, and looking to Him alone, the doubtful hesitating step of the pilgrim is reassured, and he goes on his way rejoicing. Mark the confidence of Paul's personal feelings when he finds occasion to impart them to us, "I know whom I have believed, and am persuaded that he is able to keep that which I have committed unto him.—For me to live is Christ, but to die is gain." This is the language of a man who has laid aside for ever the doubt of his acceptance with God, the doubt of Christ's ability to save to the uttermost, the doubt of his Master's constant presence and guiding spirit. By whatever means Paul had arrived to certainty on these three subjects, he never permitted any reasoning, or any knowledge subsequently acquired, to shake that certainty. Doubts on other matters arising in the progress of his ministry he would discuss in their proper time, but those which had once been disposed of, were forgotten for ever.

What a melancholy religion is theirs who are ever contending with old doubts. It is as if they were always asking, "Who art thou, Lord?" For after the Lord has showed them His hands and His side, to assure their hearts that He is the very Sacrifice that has borne their sins; after they have seen Him with the eye of faith, after they have looked upon, and their hands have handled of the Word of Life, they seem unable to let this matter rest as an established immutable fact: a conversation with an unbeliever, the perusal of a book, the pressure of a besetting sin, disturbs their assurance, and they go over the old ground, "Who art thou Lord? Art thou my very Saviour? Tell me again my peace is made. Tell me in clearer tones, and with shining evidence that Thou art mine!" And the tones become once more audible, the still small voice of heavenly love—"O thou of little faith, wherefore didst thou doubt? I have engraved thee on the palms of my hand!" Ah! that was so expressly, so distinctly spoken, they can never doubt again. Oh that they could always feel as they do now! But, my brethren, it is not given to us to feel at all times alike, so when their feelings change, their doubts recur, and the old conflict begins again. Whereas, having obtained faith in Jesus, the faith that justifies them, and by which they are adopted into the family of God,—a transaction, let me say, that rests upon the oath, the covenant oath, of Him who cannot lie,—they ought to give all diligence to add to their faith courage to confess it, to avow it to themselves and to their brethren.

A bold utterance of our trust in Jesus is an excellent remedy for unbelieving fears. To this boldness of confessing Christ, they should add knowledge: they should go on to know the Lord. A growing knowledge of Christ will multiply instances of His faithfulness, and make the believer acquainted with the diversity of his manifestations to the heart, and with the inherent sweetness and loveliness of His Person. Knowledge will thus fortify both faith and courage. And then, lest knowledge should puff up, there should follow temperance, self-discipline, meek endurance under adverse circumstances, and to all these there should be added a habit of fervent piety to God and charity to men.

Such is the masterly discrimination of the degrees of a Christian's progress given us by St. Peter in his second Epistle. He that lacketh these things, saith this Apostle, that is, he that stops with his first faith, adding nothing to it, is blind, he grows blind, he cannot see afar off into those things that are before, and "hath forgotten that he was purged from his old sins;"—he fails to realize his forgiveness as a fact; he dwells upon debatable ground, is never happy, and sometimes draws back unto perdition! *Let us therefore fear, lest a promise being left us of entering into God's rest, any of you should come short of it,* by failing to hold the beginning of his confidence firm unto the end.

Thus did Paul forget what he had given up for Christ; thus did he forget also the errors and doubts that marked his first approaches to Christ; and the rudiments of his Christian experience.

We have seen what Paul left behind: let us now come up to the front and look into the distance for a glimpse of the things towards which Paul is running, and reaching as he runs. The phrase " reaching forth," is beautifully consistent with the image of " a runner whose body is bent forward in his course." What those things were which the Apostle so eagerly and strenuously pursued, may be summed up in one expression, *a perfect fellowship with Christ*—He followed after, that he might lay hold of this, for which he had been laid hold of by Christ himself—" That I may know him," said this passionate admirer of his Lord, " and the power of his resurrection, and the fellowship of his sufferings, being made conformable unto his death, if by any means I might attain unto the resurrection of the dead."

Perhaps few knew more of Christ than did Paul when he wrote these words; yet he considered his attainments but as the first steps in a path of ever unfolding discovery. Jesus was a mine he had just opened; and he describes his prospects like a man almost bewildered by the sudden inheritance of wealth untold. He had always reckoned himself one with his Master; but this oneness grew upon him, as if Paul's personality would disappear in the overlaying and absorbing nature of the infinite Christ; for not only did he feel that the power that raised Christ from the dead was making him like Christ, and that the new spirit that bounded within him was the life of Christ, and that the suffering he endured was the dying of the Lord Jesus, but he was conscious that these feelings of participation displayed to his hope a yet deeper fellowship. Every studious thought upon Jesus was followed by a brighter manifestation of his character; every affliction that befel the Apostle seemed to bind him by another cord to the heart of the great Sufferer. He longed to master the profound problem of pain: the sin that brought it into the world, the love that adopted it and made it a holy thing, and the glory that lay beyond it.

The things after which Paul was ever reaching were mysteries of fellowship with Jesus. To win Christ, was not, in Paul's sense, to gain His favour simply, but to be conformed to His image; to go down to His lowliness and rise with His majesty; to taste pangs of dishonor or physical distress, if such awaited him, that he might the more exquisitely sympathize with *the agony and bloody sweat, the cross and passion:* to enter with his Leader and elder Brother into the dark arena where principalities and powers were to be overcome, to defeat their forces, to level their strongholds to the dust : to be with his Lord in the sublime strife of battle, until with the Ark of his strength the conqueror entered into his rest. REST! that was Paul's crown: the rest of perfect fellowship with Him of the many crowns,—one in matchless purity of mind, one in undying love for each other, one in a transfigured body with the MAN by whom came the resurrection of the dead, one in the administration and honors of that kingdom which is world without end.

SERMON II.

Isaiah vi. 1—4.

"In the year that King Uzziah died I saw also the Lord sitting upon a throne, high and lifted up, and his train filled the temple. Above it stood the seraphims: each one had six wings; with twain he covered his face, and with twain he covered his feet, and with twain he did fly. And one cried unto another, and said, Holy, holy, holy, is the Lord of hosts: the whole earth is full of his glory. And the posts of the door moved at the voice of him that cried, and the house was filled with smoke."

OBSERVE the date of this vision, "In the year that King Uzziah died." Uzziah is supposed by some writers to have been the uncle of the prophet. It is certain that Isaiah was a kinsman of the royal family; and the death of a relative so illustrious and venerable must have made a deep impression upon the young prophet's mind. Uzziah, moreover, had been a great friend to the people of God. For two and fifty years he had striven to preserve Judah from idolatry, while Israel was rent asunder by the wickedness and shameful misrule of a succession of the most abandoned monarchs that ever polluted a throne. Isaiah, whom God had early called into his service, could not but regard the death of Uzziah as a heavy misfortune both to Judah and Israel, and he probably apprehended dark days for the people of God. It was at this time that the desponding prophet was favoured with the vision of the seraphim, in which were shadowed forth the future purposes of God.

The scene of the vision is laid in the temple. We must suppose Isaiah to be standing in the inner court, beside the altar of burnt-offering, at the entrance of the building. The doors are opened, the veil is drawn aside, and the holiest apartment of the tabernacle is disclosed to the prophet's eye. At the end, where the ark was placed, and above the figures of the cherubim, high and lofty, sat Jehovah, in majesty, surrounded by the angelic host. The temple was filled with His train, the ample and flowing light which, like the skirts of a robe, He drew after him.

The elevation of the throne, *high and lifted up*, represents the unrivalled supremacy of God's rule. With regard to all government He is emphatically the " high and lofty one." All powers and forces that spread themselves abroad over the universe; those silent authorities that keep the stars in their places and extend their ministry to the minutest wants of the creation; those mighty elements of the human breast,—intelligence, will, valour and ambition, which make and unmake kings, build up and demolish empires; and that diviner control which the good and the gentle have over the wicked' and the untamed,—all these agencies, the peaceful and the troublous, the evil and the propitious, the mighty and the feeble, lie far below the footstool of the Eternal Throne, and hold their power in pliant deference to His will. At so sublime a height, how appropriate is the posture of the King of kings, *sitting*. "I saw the Lord sitting upon a throne." This implies the composure of Almighty power. To Him who knows all things there can be no surprise; to Him who governs all things, no disturbance. The influences that fret and fume beneath, in a world that knows no tomorrow; the boastings of evil men, the quakings and sufferings of the good; vice lording it over virtue, and superstition triumphing over knowledge; the disastrous tumults of war, the desolations of epidemics, the prosperity of oppression and knavery,—all phenomena that perplex and confound good men, are only the chafings and lashings of existence on the shores of Time, while the tide is changing, but in the eternal deep all is calm. The Psalmist found consolation from the same thought, when he saw the fierce raging and profane plottings of God's enemies, "He that *sitteth* in the heavens shall laugh, the Lord shall have them in derision."

Notice the description of the seraphim, His attendants. "Above it," above Him, "stood the seraphims; each one had six wings; and with twain he covered his face, and with twain he covered his feet, and with twain he did fly." It is unnecessary for me to prove that the existence of good and evil angels is a doctrine of the Bible, but it may be useful, before approaching the details of Isaiah's vision, to gather from the divine Word some account of those pure and elevated beings that stand in the presence or execute the will of God.

Referring to their number, Daniel describes thousand thousands ministering unto the Ancient of days, and ten thousand times ten thousand standing before him. Paul speaks of "an innumerable company of angels;" and similar testimonies will be found in the Psalms. As regards their office, we learn that they accompany the Divine Majesty and the Saviour, and take part in all critical displays of judgment and mercy. God spake through His angels when the law was delivered on burning Sinai. Angels followed the Saviour when He destroyed Jerusalem; and their bright and gorgeous ranks will be summoned to heighten the pomp of the judgment. We learn, moreover, that angels are the guardians of individuals and of nations. They heralded the birth of Christ, were present on the great occasions of His life, ministered to His wants, strengthened him in His conflicts, watched over His tomb, announced His triumphant resurrection, and returned with Him to glory. They hover round families, ministering to the saints, and holding the special guardianship of little children, "whose angels do always behold the face of our heavenly Father." So of nations. In Daniel the angel Michael is styled the prince of the Jews, the great prince who standeth for the people of God. An angel is represented in this book as struggling with the Prince of Persia for the liberation of the Jews. Michael appears again in Zechariah, rebuking Satan for his malignant intentions towards Joshua the High Priest. Even the elements seem to be placed under the superintendence of angels. John, in the Revelation, saw four of these spirits holding the four winds of the earth. There is mention also of an angel who presided over the fire, and another is designated the angel of the waters. The Jews had a vivid impression of the doctrine of angelic existences, and their writings abound in minute and familiar descriptions of these heavenly ministers.

Returning to the *seraphim* of the vision, let us notice some particulars in Isaiah's sublime description. Their mysterious figures were seen standing above, or on either side of the Divine Majesty. Each one had six wings. We presume that their form was that of a man, for naturally we can connect the intellect with no other image. The wings must indicate additional powers. What these attributes are, it is not easy to find. Wings are emblematical of fleetness and obedience. The two that shaded the face appear to have branched from the head, as symbolic of great swiftness of thought: an intelligence that does not arrive at a conclusion by the tedious process of inductive experiment, but alights upon it as from above; an understanding at once prompt, rapid, and luminous. Active and hard thinking wears out a man; but activity is the natural posture of an angel's mind; and knowledge, deep, high and various, is its exhilarating aliment. The most acute and fortunate inquirers among us, are generally men who bend their attention to one subject, and any success they may reap is the hard fruit of a life's study. But the strong and nimble wing of an angelic intelligence can range from subject to subject, and cover, as it were, a whole system of truth at once. The Psalmist says that God maketh his angels a flame of fire, or lightning; alluding, probably, to the quick flashing of thought and suddenly comprehensive knowledge here indicated by the wings that grew from the head of the seraphim. But these head-wings were folded in the presence of the Divine Majesty. "With twain he covered his face." There is something peculiarly expressive and touching in a seraph shading his face before his Maker—the swift and mighty intellect drew back before the piercing and awe-inspiring eye of the Eternal, as if it feared to meet the blaze of that countenance which illumines heaven! The lofty seraph feels that he is a poor creature in the presence of God; a mere insect, flitting in the sunshine of Deity. Holy and profound as he is, he folds his wings over his mind, as if there were nothing there worthy to attract or interest his Creator.

With twain he covered his feet. Wings spreading from the feet are intended to illustrate service that is rapid in execution and complete in performance. The seraphim were waiting before God to receive His messages and to fulfil His commands; but while they stood before Him, they covered their feet to show how deeply unworthy they felt to be admitted into the Divine counsels, and how tardy and imperfect the obedience which even their feet rendered to the high and lofty One, "in whose sight the heavens are not clean, and who charges his angels with folly." The image teaches us that their conceptions of perfection far surpass their actual experience. The habitual contemplation of the absolutely perfect, makes them sensible of the diminished lustre of their best performances. Behold these glorious spirits standing in the presence of the Highest with their faces and their feet veiled, incapable of sin and yet abashed; holy, yet ashamed! Behold them ye, who in the same presence are yet unhumbled; who, without reverence or sincerity, enter the divine sanctuary, and all guilty as you are, pronounce the name of God! who kneel before the King of kings and offer Him a posture instead of a prayer!

And with twain he did fly. Angels are

ever passing from element to element, from world to world, with a swiftness which may exceed even our ideas of electric dispatch. A deep reverence folded the head-wings and the foot-wings, but there was no shame to gather up the wings of obedience; these were ever spread for service. The spirit of the seraphim shrank from the scrutinising light that emanated from the throne, and a knowledge of their imperfections admonished them not to vaunt those active powers which they employed for the fulfilling of the divine commands; but their *zeal* was ever displaying itself. The wings that were free and restless, and which their deeply loving nature prompted them to wave before their Sovereign, indicated the ardour and delight of their obedience. Their manner was not that of a servant who awaits the call of his master, and must be awakened to attention. With twain they did *fly*, or rather did *hover* about the throne before the command was issued. Their attitude showed that they had begun to obey; they had finished the preliminaries of flight before they received a command, that not a thought might elapse between law and obedience. These Princes of Heaven, gifted and mighty, seemed to remember only that they were subjects and servants. How significant the prayer, "Let thy will be done in earth, as it is done in heaven." The very Lord before whom these angels stood, taught us to pray thus! Let us make this prayer our study that it may be answered in our obedience. What poverty of love, what coldness of zeal, what weakness of decision in the service we render to God. Far from being on the wing to fly for God when His cause demands it, we are either sleeping, or serving ourselves; perhaps walking in a forbidden path, or pressing after a forbidden object. Angels wait before God; but we must be called, entreated, urged, chastised, before we can obey. And after all, there is so much murmuring and reluctance, so much half-heartedness, that the Holy Ghost fitly compares our works to *filthy rags*. How amazing the patience of the pure and lofty One, that He can bear with us at all; that even His patience is not exhausted by our indolence and unfaithfulness!

Let us now consider the *anthem* of the seraphim, "And one cried unto another and said, Holy, holy, holy is the Lord God of Hosts; the whole earth is full of His glory." Bearing in mind the subject of the vision, the Lord sitting upon a throne high and lifted up, with His glorious train filling the temple, and His princes and nobles attending Him, you will observe that Jehovah was about to perform a great work, and that the song of the seraphim was its consecrating hymn. The work in contemplation was the enlargment of His Church. He had been wont to dwell in the Jewish temple; he now proposed to fill the world with His glory. To give the prophet a type of this manifestation was the purport of the vision. Returning to the anthem, it seems to have been sung after the manner of Jewish choristry. The singers of the temple were divided into choirs; each served a week in succession, and on grand occasions they were united and sang in alternate response. The seraphim are represented as singing in three choirs. "They cried one to another, and said, Holy, holy, holy is the Lord of hosts." The word "Holy" might have been chanted by each choir separately, and the last words, "the whole earth is full of His glory," by the three choirs united. It has been supposed, and with great probability, that the division of the song, and especially the trinal repetition of "Holy," reveals the doctrine of the Trinity. The same remarkable emphasis upon *three* is found in other divine songs, as, for instance, the anthem of the four living creatures, in the Revelation, who rest not day nor night, saying, "Holy, holy, holy, Lord God Almighty, which was, and is, and is to come." The theme of this grand strain harmonizes exquisitely with the other parts of the scene. The Lord was sitting on a throne high and lifted up; within His hand was every rein of power; He could fix, He could change; He could create, He could destroy; then how vastly important to learn the nature of a Being by whom all things subsist, and what confidence is inspired, when it is announced that He is HOLY: for it implies that no sinful or wicked inclination can be found in the Almighty. As St. James affirms, "God cannot be tempted with evil;" and St. John with great solemnity gives it to the Church as a message which he had heard from Christ, that "God is light, and in him is no darkness at all." Holiness implies, moreover, that God never chooses a false way. David testifies that "as for God, his way is perfect." Some of His paths are a great deep; His measures are inexplicable, but we must conclude them just; for the nature, the internal disposition from which they spring, is holy. God not only appears just when he is understood, but he *is* just when he is not understood.

It is remarkable that while in the songs of

the Redeemed the love of God is celebrated, the holiness and equity of God inspire the hymns of angels; for these are ever employed in conducting or reporting the judgments and mercies of the divine government. They are constant witnesses of the benevolence, veracity, and justice of God; and are ever lighting upon some new aspect of the divine holiness. We may sympathize with the awful reverence of the seraphim, and though at a great distance, and in the dust, join them in *praising God at the remembrance of His holiness.*

The rapt and astonished prophet, as he listened to the seraphic notes, filling the high arches of the temple with strange echoes, and every echo repeating "Holy, holy, holy," must have justified God in his heart, in all the severities He had brought upon Israel; the judgments which had so often laid waste their lands, scattered their families, and multiplied their slain: and as his eye sought the future, and beheld greater afflictions in store for them, the warlike Babylonian, and the spoiler from Chaldea desolating his country, and tearing asunder the fellowships and hearts of his people, carrying their tribes away, away—into the land of the stranger; even before this gloomy vision he could hardly have forborne to repeat after the choir, *Holy, holy is the Lord of Hosts!* But when behind the cloud of the captivity, and yet further on in the perspective of the vision, arose the glad days of the Messiah; that Redeemer who would open the gates of Paradise to the Gentiles, and make them a people, who were not a people, and call them beloved who were not beloved; that illustrious Light and Desire of nations, whose doctrines would shine upon the remotest lands and bless the habitations of all who sit in the region of the shadow of death;—gazing upon the splendours of this prophecy with a power of realization that made every promise an accomplishment, we can imagine the rapture with which this favoured Seer would join the chorus of the anthem, *The whole earth is full of His glory!* So when the Christian is astonished at some menacing cloud, which with stern and irresistible current is sailing towards him, and he feels that, ere long, he will be enveloped in afflictions, let him not stagger! Even over that cloud angels have sung, Holy, holy, holy! and if he look beyond, piercing its dense vapour by a ray of faith, he will see the light of salvation coming after, and the promise of an abundant entrance into glory; and as he listens, the chorus of the song will break in rapturous notes upon his ear, "The whole earth is full of his glory." So the missionary, whose days and nights are consumed in the toil of preaching and teaching; when he sees no fruit of his wasted strength, when neither the books he circulates, nor the addresses he delivers, nor the schools he superintends, nor the examples he holds up, make any impression upon the benighted ones for whom he has vowed to live and die, he knows that over that cloud angels have sung, *Holy is the Lord of Hosts.* He knows that if he look behind that portentous darkness, he shall greet a coming dawn! yes, for India: a dawn for the Bramin, for the Mahomedan, for the Pariah, when these who now sit in darkness shall see a great light, and the powers, the tremendous powers of idolatry shall be shaken; when Bel shall bow down, and Nebo shall stoop, and Puranums and Shasters shall follow them to the dust; and as he listens, the chorus of the seraphic anthem shall resound from floor to roof, and from pillar to pillar, through arches and aisles of the great temple of God's universal church, *The whole earth is full of His glory!*

But the vision does not end here. "The posts of the door moved at the voice of him that cried, and the house was filled with smoke." Here was afforded to the prophet a type of the Divine work which the angelic hymn had consecrated. The chanting of superhuman voices produced a concussion within the building, and the firm and massive supports of the temple entrance shook; to intimate that God was about to break up the fixtures of the Jewish economy; that their priesthood and institutes were doomed. Temples and establishments are too contracted for the catholic chorus of the seraphim; "The whole earth is full of his glory." It seemed as if the triumphant music was impatient within walls. The great temple of Jerusalem, the idol of Jewish architecture, the grandest pile that genius ever raised, trembled like a leaf in the blast! trembled under what? not under heaven's storms, but heaven's melody! So rocked the Jewish state when the mighty Spirit put a new song into the mouths of three thousand on the day of Pentecost: the music of souls redeemed burst the enclosures of caste and language; the joyous notes forced themselves into the world without, and winged their heavenly ways to the uttermost parts of the earth and of the sea,

"The dwellers in the vales and on the rocks
Shout to each other; and the mountain tops

From distant mountains catch the flying joy:
Till nation after nation taught the strain,
Earth rolls the rapturous Hosanna round."

The prophet's dream darkens. He heard the anthem, he felt the concussion of the structure, he looked for an explanation of so uncommon a result of music: but *the house is filled with smoke.* "It is the glory of God to conceal a thing." While He is filling the earth with the light and beauty of His truth, and has made His angels spirits, and His ministers a flame of fire, that they may run to and fro to impress the bias and the vigour of His will upon the events that happen around us, this great temple service, its glory, its anthem, its ministries, its influences, is hidden from the sense of the unbelieving world; the several divisions of it succeed each other and advance to the closing solemnity; but "Eye hath not seen, nor ear heard, neither have entered into the heart of man, the things which God hath prepared for them that love him." Men themselves, like the keys of an instrument, are unconscious of the touch of the Master and the progress of the performance, and deny the existence of what they mechanically help forward. "Where is the promise of his coming," is the sceptical taunt of those who are laboriously, but blindly, hastening that event;

like the unfortunate craftsmen employed by Noah to "work out a salvation" for the people of God, who when they had completed their task perished with their own work floating in triumph above their heads! "The secret of the Lord is with them that fear him."

SERMON III.

JOHN v. 17.

"*My Father worketh hitherto, and I work.*"

THE Jews had accused Jesus of breaking the Sabbath: He had performed on that holy day a deed of mercy; and judging Him by the technical restraints of their own law, which, as narrowly interpreted by themselves, made inaction to be the essence of Sabbath-keeping, they proceeded to enforce upon Him the usual penalty of transgressing the fourth commandment. His answer is the text, "My Father worketh hitherto, and I work." The Jews understood Him to mean that He was not under their law, but was Himself the author of law, and co-equal with the Father; and they understood Him correctly, as His subsequent words clearly show; for He proceeds, in clear and positive terms, to assert His equality with God. He kept the Sabbath by ceaseless activity which, with the Author of all things, is compatible with the profoundest rest.

The first truth suggested by the passage, is the universal presence of the Father at work. "My Father worketh hitherto." "He upholds with an energy that knows no pause the work of His creation, from hour to hour, and from moment to moment." This is a doctrine very imperfectly apprehended by the world. Men do not imagine God to be near to them in actual presence. They acknowledge Him to be the Creator, but chiefly because it relieves them of the greater difficulty of otherwise accounting for the existence of things. And when they speak of His works, they do not refer to Him in person, except by approved philosophical designations that teach those who adopt them that the *personal* existence of God is little more than a speculation. Have you remarked that when we talk of the operations of nature, we rarely mention God? We speak of laws, of causes and effects; a mode of precise expression necessary and admirable when science teaches us the relations and manner of any particular existence: but surely in our ordinary references to Divine operations we ought not to shut out the name of our Father, who is through all and in us all. In addition to this scientific concealment of God, a habit now become popular with those who have no science, there is, if I may so call it, a figurative disguise of the Divine presence. By a fiction of the imagination which began with our childhood and cleaves to us through life, we make natural objects self-acting; for the absence of a visible agent makes them appear so to a child's eye: and that which was our creed once is our phraseology now. The grand creations we invest with personality, such as the sun and the planets; the spaces and the elements we people with airy shapes of poetry and romance. These imaginations not only embellish literature, they affect our modes of thought, and where there is no positive religious sentiment they become an elegant substitute for it; they serve for the Divine Being Himself. Those who introduce Him into their conversation without shading their allusion by a figure or comment, are liable to the charge of affectation, bad taste, or something worse. I do not commend the habit of mentioning the name of God on all occasions, but I state the fact to show how sparingly and ceremoniously the recognition of our Father finds expression among us. What an impressive and touching symptom of our universal ungodliness! Here is an exact description of men as we naturally find them, " God is not in all their thoughts, there is none that understandeth, there is none that seeketh after God."

But while philosophy is studying its problems of cause and effect, evading, even in its most ultimate questions, the conclusion and acknowledgement of a God; while the popular language or rhetoric of life hides our Divine Maker behind the personal attributes with which childhood invests natural objects, let us, without being enemies either to science or to imagination, open our Bible, and look upon the works of God holding this light to our feet. We let a ray of it fall upon a flower, upon the structure of an animal, upon the strata of a rock, and we perceive not only that our Father has been there, but that He is there, and we exclaim, The work of Thy fingers! "My Father worketh hitherto." If you ask us about genera and species and the laws of variation, you confound us; we leave these matters to the observation and analysis of scientific men, whose labours entitle them to respect and gratitude, but whose discoveries shall not seduce us from the faith that gives us a truer, a more subtle sight than theirs. We cannot detect half so many qualities in an object as they can, but we see our Father at work; not in the sense of being the first cause simply, but in the present action of His power. If you tell me that the instinct of the bird leads it to pick up the grain which an accident has scattered upon the ground, is it less true that our heavenly

Father feedeth it? You may explain the visible phenomena of the whole bird-history, and trace by accurate induction all the processes of its formation; what have you done, but described the ways in which the Father displays His goodness and skill? He brings forth the bird, cherishes it, teaches it flight, feeds and guards it, until it drops on the ground, which a sparrow cannot do without His notice. David was no mean naturalist; yet when he speaks of the sustentation of animals, their natural dissolution, and the renewal of their generations he passes over the laws of these changes, and only sees the Father at work. "These wait all upon thee: that thou givest them they gather: thou openest thine hand, they are filled with good: thou hidest thy face, they are troubled: thou takest away their breath, they die, and return to their dust. Thou sendest forth thy Spirit, they are created, and thou renewest the face of the earth." This is not mere poetry: it is written in the largest spirit of science. But a higher authority than David, who wrote no poetry, and who, though He sometimes taught by parable, and did not explain all He taught, never permitted His hearers to mistake for a parable an explicit truth, in whom dwelt *all the treasures of wisdom and knowledge*, when referring to the beauty of a flower, affirms that the Father clothes it; and when bidding His disciples imitate the trustful and uncareful birds, He adds, *Your heavenly Father feedeth them.*

There is another truth, consequent upon that we have been discussing, too obvious to detain us with arguments and examples, too important to be passed over. If the Father is working around us, with His hand upon everything, following the watchfulness of His unsleeping eye, sustaining the life and consulting for the happiness of all His creatures, what a security *we* enjoy, what an assurance that everything must go well! Each one of us may claim for himself the application of the text, "My Father worketh for *me.*" He bestows on me an attention as direct and personal as if I were His sole creation. Though I frequently forget Him, I am never out of His thoughts; though I often reason absurdly, and conclude falsely, and speak ungratefully, concerning the events that daily happen to me, He is all the more tender and solicitous, like a mother humouring a pettish child, forgiving, soothing, and putting me right again. " When I consider the heavens, the moon and the stars which he has ordained," the infinity that arches over me, studded with points of light, each of which Astronomy informs me is a world, with inconceivable spaces between them; when I think that they may have populations that look as we do upon a sun and moon, that myriads of thinking beings throng the universe, I say, Can it be true, that I have a separate and particular place in the Father's heart? Do not these worlds and their vast interests drive me out of His mind? What does He now whisper to my half-sceptical heart? "The very hairs of your head are all numbered!" It is sometimes hard for me to realize the truth and substance of this wonderful revelation; for in spite of it I am often depressed by a sense, a sickening sense, of loneliness, and even, for some moments, of abandonment; then I hear the expostulation of One who knoweth my frame and remembereth that I am dust. "Why sayest thou, O Jacob, and speakest, O Israel, my way is hid from the Lord, and my judgment is passed over from my God? Hast thou not known, hast thou not heard, that the everlasting God, the Lord, the Creator of the ends of the earth, fainteth not, neither is weary? There is no searching of his understanding." Thus giveth He *power to the faint, and to them who have might He increaseth strength.* Let us appropriate these words of our elder Brother, and keep them locked up in our hearts as a charm to exorcise the foul spirit of unbelief,—I am not ALONE for the Father is with me.

The third truth contained in the passage is rather implied than expressed. The Father worketh, not because an intelligent being is necessarily active, but for some great design which the Triune God is advancing and must complete. This work, extending over many ages, may be called a second Genesis. The Jews considered that when the heavens and the earth were finished, and all the host of them, God had nothing more to do. So they interpreted the words, "On the seventh day God ended the work which he had made, and he rested from all his work." It is true that the first Genesis concluded the plan of the creation, and initiated the ancestral organization of things; but God did not then enter into the gross Sabbath of inaction. When the Creator had fixed the limits of the material universe, accomplished the number of original organisms, and diffused the elements necessary to sustain them, His primal work was done: but He rested only from the creation of matter: the Sabbath into which He entered was as full of work as the six days of the Genesis; but work of another kind, of a nobler and more enduring kind. The Spirit that moved upon formless matter must now move upon mind. Evil had come into being, and evil is to mind what chaos is to matter: angels had lost their first estate, and the fallen spirits would carry their rebellion to Paradise: the serpent would creep into that fairest retreat of innocence and bliss, and leave the venom of death in the heart of its happy inmates. Sinful and degenerate, they would beget children in their likeness: woe and death would multiply with advancing and scattered families: heaven would recede from earth, and hell would draw nearer; until the entire race of men would be in league with the powers of darkness, and God their Father would be resisted and defied, from the rising to the setting of the sun; and manifold disorders, following the apostacy, would extend to other parts of the creation. The blessed God foreknew all this when He entered upon His first Sabbath, and He graciously purposed to spend that Sabbath in winning back to Himself a lost world; in making a new heaven and a new earth, not of matter but of mind. Histories have been written to describe the fortunes of races, and the rise and fall of kingdoms. Who shall write the history of God's Sabbath-work for man? The Bible is but a chapter of it; the record will run on in the ages to come, and eternity will unroll the volume. But following the memorials of scripture from the earliest annals, how evident is a progressive design of love—the Father working in counsel; the Son in personal revelation; the Spirit in influence; and looking more closely, we observe, that the Divine Son is the centre of this second and more glorious Genesis. There is, in the words of Paul, " a gathering together in one of all things in Christ, both which are in heaven and which are on earth." From Adam to Moses, from Moses to John the Baptist, all revelations pointed to Christ; all historic events worked in the direction of the cross; all institutions were like rest-houses on a highway, they detained travellers for a while, but only to refresh them for their journey to Christ: and when the Lamb of God was lifted up, He did as He foretold, He drew all men unto Him. As all matter tends to the centre of the earth and must find it when intervening resistance is taken out of the way, so all spirit draws near to Christ; it may be hindered on its path, but it cannot rest until it be united to Him. Sinner! the Father is drawing thee to Christ: the Spirit is convincing thee of thy misery out of Christ: there is no rest, no happiness, no safety for thee, severed from Him: thou art a stone flung away from the building, a limb cut off from the body, a chord broken from the harp: as thou art, there is neither use, life, nor harmony in thee: thou art a fragment, a mere piece of the general wreck: but blessed be His Name, "My Father worketh" to gather all ruined souls together in Christ. He stoops to pick thee up, thou rejected stone; to shape, polish, and set thee in the building of God. Shall He stoop in vain? shall He draw to be yet resisted? O yield to the finger of God! He will lead thee to Jesus. In Him thou wilt lose thy sins, in Him thou wilt be strong to trample under feet the temptations that oppress thee, and to suffer the trials that befall thee: in Him thou wilt find a brother, and *a friend that sticketh closer than a brother;* and the Father will join Himself with thee by one Spirit. Listen to these marvellous words, Christ is addressing the Father, and referring to His people, "I in them and thou in me, that we may be made perfect in one." But suppose the sinner will not be drawn? There is no supposition in it, he must be drawn to Christ. His very resistance is progress to Christ. He must kneel and confess that Jesus is Lord. It is simply a question of time as to the event of his submission; but not as to the character of that submission. If he kneel not now for pardon, he must kneel on the day of judgment for acknowledgement. Every tongue will there confess Him. It will be one of His *many crowns*—the prostration and public recantation of all His enemies: a recantation that will serve Him only, not them.

All men are thus proceeding Christward. Consciously and unconsciously, the Father is drawing all the races and kingdoms of the earth to Christ. The sin of one half of the world has taken the shape of hatred and dishonor to Christ: the miseries of the other half are the fruit of an ignorance of Christ: it is the glory of the Father to work hatred into love; or where this fails, to rebuke it into submission and confession. He will take no honor to Himself but that which is given through the Son: and although He hath not cast off His people, the Jews, which He foreknew, He will come to no terms with them while they refuse to acknowledge Christ: in spite of their synagogues and their Sabbaths, their readings of Moses and their offerings, the veil is still upon their hearts, and the old curse of dispersion is still upon their families, verifying the ominous words of Christ to their ancestors, "He that hateth me, hateth my Father also." No, the Jew shall yet look upon Him whom he hath pierced, and mourn for Him as one mourneth for an only son: for our Father worketh to bring them to the cross, to graft them again into the root of Jesse, and to bind up the impenitent like an incurable branch, and consume them in *the wrath of the Lamb*. The Mahommedan race will find no mercy, notwithstanding their zeal for the unity of the Father, and the services they have rendered as instruments of Divine judgment upon idolatrous lands, while they look with scorn upon the Son of Mary! But the Father is working among them, and never so conspicuously as at this moment. He is taking away their place from among the nations: the acknowledgment of Christ is the salt of kingdoms: and the Mahommedan Empire within the last six years has been crumbling from the fragility of mere rottenness, without the possibility of another coherence. 'Tis a frightful calamity, either for a nation or a man to be without Christ; to have the confession of Him extorted at last by the Father's judgments. The Papal power, professedly Christian though it be, is built upon the rejection of Christ, and stand it cannot! The Father is even now gathering it up to lay it at the feet of His Son. He has already made it a by-word in the mouths of its own children.

By a bitter irony He is making it to taste, in a sense it never desired to know, the proper position of a Church, " My kingdom is not of this world." The papal territory is slipping from the paralysed hand of the Apostate Church, the actors of which are concluding the last scene of the most direful tragedy ever performed on the world's stage! The reason may not be known even to those who are hastening the end of the Papacy; but it is evident to such as read their Bibles. Christ is not honored in Rome; therefore the Father hath not planted her, and He is plucking her up. So will you find the worm of decay at the root of every religious institution or body that does not honor Christ even as it honors the Father. But while the Father is bringing to the triumphant Redeemer the wreck of all that is Christless, and gathering into one act of compulsory homage everything that has denied or resisted the Godhead of His Son, He is collecting for the honor of the cross other trophies, the achievements of His grace; He is gathering His elect from the four winds: He is working in the assemblies of His saints, pouring upon them His own love for souls, His own sympathy for Jesus, and a wonderful spirit of missionary zeal, to devise methods by which the salvation of the gospel can be conveyed to the hearts and homes of men. Thousands are spending their days and nights in co-operating with the Father's work, both at home and abroad. Vitality, energy, and productiveness, seem to distinguish every church that honors Jesus! Glory be to God! The Father working with us, the Redeemer shall have His own! "He shall have dominion from sea to sea, and from the river unto the ends of the earth. His name shall endure for ever, his name shall be continued as long as the sun: and men shall be blessed in him: all nations shall call him blessed. Blessed be the Lord God, the God of Israel, who only doeth wondrous things, and blessed be his glorious name for ever, and let the whole earth be filled with his glory. Amen, and Amen."

SERMON IV.

Hosea ii. 21, 22.

And it shall come to pass in that day, I will hear, saith the Lord, I will hear the heavens, and they shall hear the earth; and the earth shall hear the corn, and the wine, and the oil; and they shall hear Jezreel.

WE have in this passage a highly poetical description of the order in which the different parts of the creation are connected, and of the accumulation of their several results for the benefit of man's race, called in the text *Jezreel*, a word signifying the seed of God. Nature is here represented in a series of sympathetic and reciprocal powers, waiting upon each other, addressing and answering each other. The first power is the source and controller of the rest. God creates the first form, inspires the first life, and communicates the first motion. These powers acting upon each other, are extended and diversified by the laws of mutual dependence. So intimate is the connexion of one thing with another, that you can touch no object without moving a thousand;

the impulse glides along the chain until the most distant link feels the vibration; and hence things which are very dissimilar, and are apparently incompatible with each other, have the closest affinity. The Bible is not a scientific book, but it sometimes, as in the text, affords a divine glimpse into the profounder harmonies of nature. We have hints, instead of treatises; seeds of truth that need the skill and diligent patience of the husbandman, instead of fields already white unto the harvest.

In describing the action of certain powers upon each other, the text gives us the order in which they transmit their impression;— God, the heavens, the earth, the corn and wine, and Jezreel, or man. Of these powers, the first and last only are intelligent—God with whom the influence begins, and man with whom it ends. The intermediate agents are inanimate and subordinate. Man is the being for whom heaven and earth are moved: "I will hear the heavens," saith the Lord. But what has moved the heavens to cry out? The shouting of the earth. But what has awakened the voice of the earth? The struggling and impatient growth of the corn, the oil, and the wine. And who awaits the harvest and the vintage? Man. The ploughing, the manuring, the sowing, the planting are finished. Man has done his part: but the growth is tardy, the prospect of the reaper is overcast; then cry out the wants of man. The dealer augments his price, the buyer abridges his meal—bread! bread! is the cry, from one end of the land to the other. The needy fields are appealed to: that appeal is heard by the parched and suffocated grain: but what can the grain do? The earth gives it no moisture; but what can the earth do? The heavens hold back their showers; but what can the heavens do, until God command them to unlock their stores? Thus man beseeches the grain, and the grain prays to the soil, and the soil supplicates the heavens, and the heavens cry unto God—a chain of prayer; the answer to which is another chain, corresponding to it, link with link: I will answer the heavens, and they shall answer the earth, and the earth shall answer the corn and wine, and they shall answer Jezreel. The prayer went up by stages, climbing the different steps of the creative process until it gained the uncreated One. The wants of Jezreel cried out instinctively for the corn and wine, the corn and wine pined for the fatness of the ground, the sole supporter of their growth, and the ground thirsted for the blessing of the clouds: and as the prayer ascended, so does the answer return, halting at certain intermediate causes, and assuming at every stage a new form. The prayer, though uttered by several voices and in several seasons, was one; it was for corn and wine and oil: and the answer is one; though on its way down it puts on various shapes. When God commands the heavens to collect their vapours, the corn and wine are given in the shape of rain; when the falling shower revives the earth, the corn and wine are enclosed in the moist virtue of the ground; when this virtue penetrates the plant, and " maketh increase " of the grain and the olive, the blessings approach that development for which Jezreel has been waiting, and in which only he can understand the answer to his prayer: the answer had been long on its way to him, though he considered the prayer unanswered until the corn and wine were placed before him.

This is an epitome of the laws of Providence: and the divine scheme appears to reserve its latest and best results for the human family. It does appear an arrogant assumption that the material creation was made for us; that an infinite series of cause and effect should start from the will of God, like so many lines for the conveyance of blessing, to converge upon man. But let it be remembered that man is the only rational being on earth; and, however inferior to what he might have been, there is no animal with which we are acquainted, equal to the very worst specimen of the race. He is the image of God in many grand features; he is lord of the creation; an unworthy potentate, it is true, but still of royal birth : his immortality invests him with a grandeur that throws the heavens into the shade : one rational thought, one spiritual feeling, is, perhaps, a mightier effect of creative power than a galaxy of stars. Suppose that, beside God Himself, there was only one being who could think—but one,— and he a solitary man; his intellectual recognition of God, and mental appreciation of the Divine character, would lend dignity to the universe, and reflect a glory upon its Creator far exceeding the display of all his other wonders. But how is this illustration of man's greatness surpassed by the fact of his redemption through the Son of God! What must be the value of that spirit, to save which, God humbled Himself, and became obedient unto death. In this light it is not too much to think that man is the chief object of God's providential government. His wants are consulted first, and the requirements of other creatures are ordained with reference to him.

The laws of production and decay, the occult forces which sustain the harmony of the creation, the laws which bring the phenomena of the external world into converse with the mind, not only unite to provide for the happiness of man, but are, with a wider or narrower licence, placed under his power, and yet so placed as to correct every abuse to which his privilege may tempt him. How remarkable those words, *They shall hear Jezreel, the seed of God.* Man speaks with a voice that the elements themselves listen to and obey. He calls to the lightning, and the obsequious fire descends to place itself at his disposal; it carries his messages from one end of the earth to the other. He commands the steam; and it hastens to lay its mighty resources at his feet; he yokes it as a steed to his conveyances, and makes it traverse the ocean with his ships; it toils in his mines and in his manufactories like a slave, and decorates his palaces like an artist. *They shall hear Jezreel;* light and air, and metals and gases, with their countless followers, they flock to the sound of his voice, from above, from beneath, from afar, and shape themselves at his bidding, and run off in a thousand forms to do his pleasure; and the ministry of everything contributes insensibly to the maintenance, and terminates in the dignity and happiness of man.

But while man is the main object of Providence, God is its efficient and all pervading cause. *I will perform my part upon the heavens, and they shall perform their part upon the earth, and the earth shall perform her part upon the corn and the wine, and they shall perform their part for Jezreel.* Observe that though in these several spheres of agency, the part of God appears to be limited to the heavens, He pervades the series: His command runs through them—the heavens and the earth shall perform their part upon each other; clearly showing that the laws of their mutual action were ordained by Himself, and that His watchful eye follows up their latest results. The corn, the wine, and the oil shall perform their part for Jezreel. It is not that He establishes great laws of life and organization, and leaves their minuter applications to chance. He will superintend all their processes,—through the vapour, the shower, the vigour of the moist earth, the bursting grain in blade, ear, and full corn, the sprouting vine in tendril, leaf, and ruddy grape: He will follow all until He arrive at the rejoicing of harvest and of vintage. The eye of God is upon Jezreel—

upon *us*. When He sets in motion a blessing for us, it has to travel perhaps a long way, to pass through various processes, to wear a hundred disguises : now it sinks out of sight and seems for a while to be forgotten or abandoned; then it reappears in a new form, and bending its way in another course, as if Providence had altered its destination ; but after rejoicing those who needed it earlier than we, it returns in the direction of ourselves ; and as it draws nearer it grows every moment more adapted to our wants, until the fulness of time brings it into our happy possession. Now, during its wide, and, as we should call it, eccentric course, God never loses sight of it, and never loses sight of us. Whatever be its apparent path, it is always on its way to us; whatever be its apparent form, it is always shaping itself for us. It is not correct to call the interval of our tarrying for it a delay; there is no delay in the divine operation ; a blessing is never waiting for us, it is coming to us; and in all its stages and through all its way, it is doing good to some object, and lending itself under some form to the happiness of the universe.

The order observable in the physical world is not more immutable in its ordinance, more minute in its applications, than are the laws of the spiritual world. If these do not appear to be so strictly conditioned, it is only because we know less about them. The philosopher who finds it impossible to conceive of a single event in nature detached from established law, and concludes that no amount of testimony can make a miracle credible, may affirm with equal reason that no *moral event* can be unique, or stand unrelated to a system. It is as hard to imagine a suspension of order in the one case as in the other. And yet the miracle ought not to be a stone of stumbling to any man who believes in a God. To suppose it to be impossible, or equivalent to a contradiction of our natural sense, that God should stop the application of a law, to answer a special end, is to suppose it to be impossible that there should be a God at all. The only consistent idea of a Supreme Being is the old-fashioned scriptural notion that with God nothing is impossible; a doctrine which the simplest reader will know how to guard from those absurd consequences which modern philosophers assure us are involved in it. But to return to the order of the spiritual world. The remarks suggested by the text on the mode, government, and direction of providential operations will equally apply to the economy of grace. The human race is the seed of God. The nations that know Him not have some interest in the promise, " I will be a father unto you." But this relation He sustains with peculiar tenderness toward those who are the spiritual Jezreel, the children of His grace through the new and nobler generation of His Spirit. He is the common parent of all; but to those who believe in His Son He is the reconciled Father, and the ministry of His providence is to them the ministry of His love. The just and the unjust share in the corn and the wine and the oil; He walks through all lands, and His paths drop fatness; but those only who love Him are permitted to return with Him into His sanctuary and enjoy the easy and confiding intercourse of children. Of such it may be said that not only the blessings of the atmosphere, the soil, the ocean, and the mine are theirs, but theirs also are the riches, the forces, and the servants of the invisible world. *They shall hear Jezreel*, not material agents only, to unite in producing for him a material blessing. The chain that runs from the vapour to the corn is for the life that now is. There is another chain, descending to us through spiritual influences and revelations. The first link is hidden in the love of God; the last is the glorious salvation of man's race. It is as if God should say of these sublimer powers also, I will hear, I will hear the law, and the law shall hear the atonement of Christ, and the atonement of Christ shall hear faith, and faith shall hear Jezreel, the sinner. Through these stages, pardon has come down to me. When it first came forth from God, it was in the form of law. I did not see forgiveness in law, but there it was. To me it was a cloud of thunderings, and voices, and hailstones; but the blessing I wanted was locked up in it, and when it reappeared in the great atonement, faith discerned it and cried out for it; and it was given to faith, and faith gave it to me. God has let down this ladder to earth: we can only see the steps that are nearest us, the higher gradations are lost in intermediate clouds—lost, but not broken; they go up with an entire connexion, and lean upon the throne, and the angels of God are ascending and descending upon Jezreel, the seed of God. The sinner cries for pardon, and pardon demands faith, and faith asks for an atonement, and the atonement pleads for the approbation of law, and law is the sanction and authority of God. When we touch the link of prayer, faith is moved; and when faith is moved, the atonement is moved; and when the atonement is moved, God is moved, and the blessings glide down : they come at the bidding of Jezreel,— "they shall hear Jezreel." The Spirit hears and comes down, and places His mighty resources at our disposal. We say to Him, Go and enlighten and save that man, and He goeth; come and renovate our dying church, and He cometh, and our sanctuaries are filled with the luminous energy of His presence. Distant nations are lying hopelessly in the shadow of death; give them Thy light and Thy truth: and He takes the wings of the morning and flies to the uttermost parts of the earth and the sea; and nations start up from the sleep of ages, and walk in the light, as we are in the light. "They shall hear Jezreel;" Paul and Apollos and Cephas—the ministry are ours; their talents, gifts, and graces come at our call and minister to our salvation: the world is ours—its habitation, bounty, and lessons, as long as we shall need them: life is ours—its far more exceeding and eternal weight of glory: death is ours to lead us to that glory: things present and things to come, they all hear Jezreel; for he is Christ's, and Christ is God's.

SERMON V.

EZEKIEL i. 1.

Now it came to pass in the thirteenth year, in the fourth month, in the fifth day of the month, as I was among the captives by the river of Chebar, that the heavens were opened, and I saw visions of God.

A FIRST glance at this chapter may well discourage any attempt to make it intelligible; and perhaps no amount of pains bestowed upon the various symbols in which its meaning resides would enable us to explain them without error; but the meaning itself shines out with sufficient clearness to give us both knowledge and comfort.

In the first place, it is certain that the visions herein described are intended to teach us the nature, the manner, and the purport of God's providence. The appearances which the prophet saw were four—the cherubim, the wheels, the crystal firmament, and the throne of God. An attentive observation of these will, I think, show that they compose one picture; that the four cherubim are yoked to a crystal chariot of four wheels, and that on the chariot is placed the throne of God, who directs its path and reins its velocity. The Psalmist illustrates this thought, exalting it to a wonderful height of poetry, "He rode upon a cherub and did fly: yea, he did fly upon the wings of the wind." The omnipresent Deity is represented as moving, to give us a vivid idea of the activity of His presence and government. In various parts of the world great events are pending; that is, waiting for the fitting instrument and the fitting season,—a political crisis, a moral revolution, a scientific discovery. God passes on a cherub from the scene of one occurrence to that of another, removing impediments, collecting friendly, dispersing adverse, forces; hastening here, delaying there, now opposing, now yielding, but having every man, every animal, every element, under supreme control, and making all bend to the fulfilment of His purpose. Nothing is too mighty for His grasp, nothing is too mean for His use.

But thoughtless men, who, in matters that concern themselves, walk and judge by sense, while they are struck with admiration or terror at the power that surrounds them, are disposed to regard it as a blind force, convulsed, or hushed, as circumstances may accidentally determine the earthquake or the drought, the storm, or the many diseases that fly loosely about, some slaying their thousands, others their ten thousands; and though experience has taught us defence, and science has furnished us with weapons to contend with most evils, yet we cannot get rid of an uneasy sense of weakness and dread, when we happen to be in the neighbourhood of an explosion of some unknown power. If we fall victims to it, it is said we are unfortunate; if we escape its ravages, we are lucky. And though we seem to attribute much to caution, and the application of means, and to impute calamity to ignorance or recklessness, we always reserve, both for success and failure, a certain persuasion that the contrary might as easily have happened. What I mean is, that men find it difficult to separate from themselves the idea that the powers that drive them through life obey no master's hand, but plough up their own wild course.

The chapter before us corrects this impression. In fact, all the histories and doctrines of the holy volume refute the notion of a chance government, and explode also that more rational, but equally untrue, theory of a distant and haughty administration which would make the laws of the universe irrespective of the individual, and restricted to the class. The writings of God everywhere inculcate a particular Providence: they reveal the tender economy of a parent; the Father who feeds, clothes, instructs, and guards his "little ones;" a doctrine full of comfort, though few can taste it. To apply it to another's distress is easy; to extract from it balm for one's own misery demands a strong effort of faith. It is a lesson to be rehearsed every hour, and practised in every trial. No doctrine is so often required, or so readily forgotten. Hence it is taught in almost every page of the Bible—in narratives and songs, in expositions and symbols; it is illustrated for the child, reasoned out for the philosopher, and exemplified for the saint.

Ezekiel delivered his prophecies in Babylon, and saw his first visions on the banks of the Chebar. He and his countrymen were captive Jews, and the prophet was one of the few who did not hang their harps on the willows. He was commanded to say, in effect, to his fellow prisoners, that Nebuchadnezzar's triumph over them—his insolence, sacrilege, and cruelty—was not an accidental issue of war, but a judgment from heaven for their crimes; that their conqueror had been executing the Divine will; and that God, who had so strangely reduced them to this humiliation, could as strangely and as unexpectedly reinstate them in a new Jerusalem, and recover the splendour which Babylon had insulted and eclipsed. Ezekiel has embodied these instructions in the imagery of this chapter, in which we are taught the attributes, the methods, and the ends of the divine Providence.

The attributes of Providence may be gathered from the description of the cherubim. The prophet has sketched four figures. They are exactly alike; and an outline of one, as clear as I can make it, will serve for the rest. I introduce nothing fanciful, but present to you, as faithfully as a very careful attention may enable me, the image which the Holy Ghost has drawn for our learning, and which will be found rich in instruction and comfortable suggestion to the simplest mind that will devoutly study it.

Imagine a creature in stature and uprightness of form like a man; in almost every other respect differing from a man. Instead of a man's head you behold four faces; the face of a man and the face of a lion looking on the right side; and the face of an ox and the face of an eagle looking on the left side. Bringing our eye downward from the faces, we see four wings: two on one shoulder and two on the other, being so placed as that one might fall below the other; the higher pair of wings branching off from opposite shoulders are for flight; the lower wings are probably intended to lap over each other as a raiment or covering for the body. Between the wings we discern the hands of a man. The overwrapping wings guide the eye to the feet, and these are very remarkable: the legs are straight and rigid, terminating in a cloven hoof, like the foot of a calf. You must imagine these hoofs, not misshapen and worn by toil, but symmetrical—hard, and polished like brass.

Look first at the faces of the cherubim. They exhibit the moral character of Providence. God governs us with intelligence and sympathy, for there is *a human face*. The figure, with its strange and apparently inconsistent formation, came forth from the whirlwind the fire and the cloud, appalling the gaze of the prophet; but when he saw a human face he knew he had nothing to fear. When we are surprised by the suddenness of a visitation, and dismayed by what appear to be eccentric and uncertain judgments, revolving around us like the huge wheels of the prophet, and glancing at us from all points, if a man's face looks out from amongst them, it charms away the terror; it seems to say, "It is I be not afraid;" as if we had a brother there in the midst of those dread elements; if there be a face, there is a heart somewhere. This is the Deity of the vision, the God-man who seems to say, "When thou passest through the waters, I will be with thee; when thou walkest through the fire, thou shall not be burned; neither shall the flame kindle upon thee." Thank God for the *human heart* that lies within the divinity of His providence! His steps are in the deep, His councils are hidden in a cloud, and His judgments smite and scatter like the lightning; but there is sympathy for man in all; the familiar face of a brother gladdens the storm like a rainbow. It is the welcome sign of the covenant that God will not always chide, neither keep His anger for ever.

As to the other faces, they prefigure qualities in which man is defective. The vision has reference to our impression of man. The human countenance cheers us with the recognition of brotherhood; but experience has warned us that in seasons of danger man's arm is impotent to save; that in the carrying out of large and difficult measures, he lacks perseverance; that in particular crises, where everything depends on accurate judgment or daring action, he lacks penetration and promptitude. Now, in the cherubim, the faces of the lion, ox, and eagle are joined to that of man, and signify that, while love and sympathy are the reigning attributes of Providence, there is power to destroy and to deliver, typified in the face of the lion; there is constancy and firmness suggested by the hard and sober face of the ox; there is unerring foresight and swiftness of perception depicted in the emblem of the eagle. Here then, are firmness, foreknowledge, power, and love; and love is the inspiration of all! And as the prophet saw four cherubim, whose faces and wings all answer to the description we have given, it is implied that the attributes prefigured by one of them are infinite, being illustrated by four: four, in symbolic language, is a perfect number; so that firmness, typified in one of the faces of each of the four figures, is firmness in every direction—that is, immutability; so foresight in every direction is omniscience; power in every direction is omnipotence; and love in every direction is the love of God!

Two other particulars must now engage our attention. There are wings for the highest heaven, there are feet to touch the earth.

The laws and blessings of Providence cannot be dispensed with in the angelic world; and they stoop even to us; not simply to touch us, to make a faint impression on us, but to dwell with us, doing the meanest offices for us; disdaining no attention and shrinking from no task that our condition requires. This condescension has a remarkable type in the cherubim's feet, which were like the feet of a calf, cloven and shaped to sink into the earth, to plod and toil under burdens over many a weary way. The idea is, that Providence is with us in our homestead: the foot of a calf is a domestic image; the divine government embraces within its care the interests, and lifts upon its back the burdens and sorrows of life. But we do not press too heavily on Providence; neither does Providence, by treading so deeply in earth, contract any of its defilement. The prophet says that the hoofs of the cherubim sparkled like the color of burnished brass. No impurity could cleave to them, no labour could misshape them. God causes a divinity to sparkle even from the foot of His administration. Those natures that seem most distant from Him, those concerns that appear to be too trivial for His regard, are permitted to manifest His glory.

The other circumstance to be noticed is the motion of the cherubim. "And they went every one straight forward: whither the Spirit was to go, they went; and they turned not as they went." Two things are remarkable:—First: One spirit animated them all—faces, wings, feet—all the intelligence, feeling, and power which they imply, were governed by one impulse, and, of course, acted together in perfect harmony. The natures being naturally antagonistic, we should expect the man to look contemptuously on the foot of the calf, and say, I have no need of thee; the lion to disdain a union with the ox; and the eagle to be impatient of a yoke that kept him from his native skies; and again, the man to proudly disown a fellowship with cattle and birds. Moreover, when we look at one of these figures, so unnaturally made up of faces, wings, hands, and feet, our taste is shocked. Why four faces, when one would be sufficient? And if there be wings to fly, why the hoofs of a beast of burden? There is no keeping, no fitness in the disposition of the figure. It is a mass of contradiction! Such, according to our maxims of drawing and taste, is the impression of the beholder when he first looks upon the cherubim. But the prophet bids us examine further; and we see that these opposite natures and dispositions, the low and the high, the sluggish and the swift, cleave together with the concord of mutual dependence and under the inspiration of one motive. Providence is an administration whose outward features may be apparently inimical or opposed to each other; and short-sighted man has felt himself at liberty to complain of strange contradictions in the Divine government. For example: one intimation to Herod would have averted the Bethlehem massacre. Is this consistent with "Suffer little children to come unto me?" Again: how can the Divine benevolence agree with the permission of so long a reign of error and wickedness? If God really loves men, and the gospel is His regenerating instrument, why does He not place it beyond the doubt of the sceptic, the false faith of the idolator, and the powerful enmity of "high places?" Why should the isles wait so long for salvation, and the ends of the earth lie many ages under the thraldom of superstition? Why should the gospel plod on like the ox, when it has wings to fly like the eagle? Again: if Providence be the affectionate economy of a father, why does He, without an apparent reason, descend like a terror into the families of His people, withering the fairest flowers of their house, and disturbing or plucking up the deepest roots of their attachment? Why should the eye and fangs of the lion flash upon us and devour us in the path of goodness and mercy?

These arrangements of the Divine government do not accord with man's wisdom. *He* would have constructed a system in which virtue would be of easier attainment, and better guarded: in which the triumph of just principles would not be delayed, and the defeat and ruin of the kingdom of sin would be summary. But, as in the many-shaped cherubim of the prophet, so in God's many-featured government, mercy and truth meet together, righteousness and peace kiss each other. One spirit animates and reconciles them all; it is the spirit of omniscient love: this element penetrates every pore of the Divine administration; it balances all inequalities, expounds all severities, sheds a grateful and guiding light upon the most intricate passages of life, making its very deserts blossom, transmuting its basest materials into gold, and winning from its harshest and most discordant notes an anthem of praise to God!

Secondly: the Spirit that animated the cherubim impelled them straight forward, neither turning back nor halting; and the wheels followed them, planted with eyes for every direction of vision. So does Omniscient love move directly to its object; we cannot see its line; the subtle thread eludes an angel's eye; but let us be sure that the track is unerringly preserved; its course may lead through floods and deaths, but these cannot change it, it is love still,—love in the martyr's flame, love in the racking disease, in the desolating bereavement, in the closing agonies of dissolution! Brethren, we have nothing to dread from the conduct of Providence. Those occurrences which happen independently of us are under the wise and gentle authority of our Father in heaven. We must not call them *visitations* of God, as if He descended upon us to punish and affright us, and then left us in precarious repose until our sins or His pleasure should prompt Him to resume His judgments. He does not *visit* us, He is always with us. *I will never leave you.* And if the doubt recurs to us, as it naturally may, whether an infinite and spiritual Being can make His universal eye to rest with keen and sympathetic attention on us; whether the Hand that rounded and lit up the heavens can perform little ministries for us, like those of the mother and the nurse—for us, who in His presence are as the drop of a bucket;

whether it is possible for me to reckon Him who inhabiteth eternity as an inmate of my house; as presiding, unseen, at my table; as looking with even more tenderness and solicitude than I, upon the members of my family, contriving little changes and incidents, in seasons and ways unknown to me, to make me and mine happy; as never at any time absent from us, and especially near in seasons of trial, to do for us *more than we can ask or think:* if, I say, we are tempted to doubt whether God had so intimate a knowledge of us, so affectionate and pervading a government over us, let it be remembered that He who reigns over us has become one of us. We have been describing the cherubim, the wheels, and the crystal firmament resting on them and borne on by them; but whom did the prophet see sitting on the top, the ruling Majesty of all? He affirms that he saw the appearance of a man enthroned, and that the glory around Him was like the appearance of the bow in the cloud in the day of rain. This is the exalted Redeemer, whom John afterwards beheld in the Apocalypse, whose eyes were like a flaming fire, whose feet were like unto burning brass, whose voice was as the sound of many waters.

Let the afflicted soul look up, and discern

through the terrible majesty of the throne the human heart of Christ, taking part with the infirmities, temptations, and sorrows of His people. That inner wheel of events which men so much dread, should have no terror for them that are His, whose touch impresses its revolutions, whose gentle wisdom determines its course. It executes designs of love; for it begins with love—the sacrifice of Himself for sinners: and it ends with love—the recovery of a lost world to God; and all the intermediate events, personal and collective, are pressed into the service of love. The purpose of God reigns in every incident; as these occur in order, they silently communicate to each other the impulse of the Divine will; there is not a chance or disorderly circumstance amongst them. Human nature, in its absolute ignorance of results, and in its impatience under suffering, may find it hard to repress the murmur, "These things are against me;" but after the struggle is over, murmuring is changed into thankfulness,— *I will glory in tribulations also.—Before I was afflicted I went astray, but now I have kept thy word.* We sometimes think God is dealing heavily with us; one trial follows another, with no space to breathe between; there seems to be a union of afflicting circumstances, all concurring to distress and weigh us down. Whichever way we turn, some weapon is pointed against us. We are ready, like Job, to curse the day of our birth. We are tempted, like the hunted prophet, to beseech God to take us away. But let me remind you of the Man of Sorrows. Can you imagine a blacker desolation than that which hung over the Saviour when He lay prostrate and alone in the garden of Gethsemane? Was the countenance of His Father changed towards Him in that saddest hour? Was it because the purpose of love hesitated, that the Son of God was abandoned to murderers, and, as it were, to the torments of the lost? Nay, even these harsh and revolting instruments were obeying the counsels of love. The triumphs of Pentecost were sown in the humiliations of Calvary. *He that goeth forth and weepeth, bearing precious seed, shall doubtless come again with rejoicing, bringing his sheaves with him.*

SERMON VI.

MATTHEW xxviii. 16—20.

"*Then the eleven disciples went away into Galilee, into a mountain where Jesus had appointed them. And when they saw him, they worshipped him: but some doubted. And Jesus came and spake unto them, saying, All power is given unto me in heaven and in earth. Go ye therefore, and teach all nations, baptizing them in the name of the Father, and of the Son, and of the Holy Ghost; Teaching them to observe all things whatsoever I have commanded you: and, lo, I am with you alway, even unto the end of the world. Amen.*"

THERE must certainly have been present more than the eleven apostles on this mountain in Galilee where Jesus had appointed to show Himself to His followers. It is not unlikely that this was the occasion when above five hundred brethren* assembled to satisfy themselves of the reality of His resurrection, and to receive some memorable token of it before His departure. It must have been a sublime spectacle,—five hundred on the top of a mountain, and Jesus in their midst, radiant with

1 Cor. xv. 6.

victory over sin, death, and hell, and, in the presence of the surrounding company, taking possession of all things! Above was the heaven; and He laid His hand upon its light and upon its space, and the infinite secrets locked up in it; below lay the earth and the fulness thereof, all the kingdoms of the world and the glory of them, which Satan, whom He was now dragging at His chariot wheels, once offered Him; He gathered them all up within the deed of His right and the capacity of His hand, all their mind and matter; and as He thus stood, "far above all principality and power, and might, and dominion, and every name that is named," He announced His position, "All power is given unto me in heaven and in earth. Go ye therefore, and teach all nations, baptizing them in the name of the Father, and of the Son, and of the Holy Ghost; and lo, I am with you alway, even unto the end of the world."

Observe the authority which this command receives from the position of Christ. *All power is given unto me;* go therefore, and convert the world. Think of *power* according to the impressions we have received of it, and then think of Jesus possessing all power. We have but a very indefinite idea of power. The forces of nature come but partially and reluctantly within the range of our knowledge, and give dreadful hints of what remain behind. We have now and then a glimpse of power, as it moves on its way to do the bidding of the Omnipotent; but from an imperfect glance of its course, we cannot conjecture its errand. The particular effect we may happen to see is not final, and may not be analogous to that which is final. The thunderbolt that blasts the Indian's hut is to him final. He cannot look beyond his loss; and he sees an angry god in the clouds, or hears him in the wind. The man of science greets the storm, and sees a benign providence in atmospheric convulsions; for, looking beyond himself into the broad field of result, he discovers that they are not sent to destroy men's lives, but to save them. But the philosopher becomes in his turn untutored: the power in the storm leaves him with the knowledge of a good issue, and holds on its trackless way to distant and unknown regions of effect. We cannot doubt that all things in nature work together for good; but we cannot by any one event learn in what manner or in what degree that good has been promoted.

When by any means we can bring power near to us in the form of steam, electricity, or heat, so as to compare it with our own tiny arm, how wonderfully sublime its presence and image! like its original, fearful in our praises, doing wonders. Stand in the engine-room of a manufactory, and let the wheels and pistons of the great power move, and you collect the strength of an army of men. By mastering the conditions upon which some great element can be reproduced and governed, man multiplies his own power indefinitely, as you may see in the marvels of modern machinery. Follow the operations of steam, in agriculture, manufacture and transit; pursue its countless ramifications into the remote necessities of life, and think upon the fact, that we are only beginning to know its capacity and to learn its management. And so of electricity, which we have married to thought, and thus endowed with an intellectual power. Speech travels with light, and distance is forgotten: man holds daily converse with man over continents, through the depths of seas, and the bowels of the earth. Deliberations, instructions, compacts, messages, and tidings, are flying over the world; and nations of different skies, languages, and religions, are exchanging counsels with each other with the facility of men consulting in a personal interview.

I mention steam and electricity, because they have become as it were a part of ourselves. They are an incalculable augmentation of power; they have impressed their genius upon war, upon commerce, upon literature, and upon intercourse; they are beginning to decide the relative eminence of nations; they are giving their own vast scale to every movement; and perhaps they are destined to be the chief of the material instruments that shall hasten the closing revolutions of the world. Mighty as they are in themselves, when they are mated with invention and passion, their power becomes appalling! Let us follow them as they become the allies of thrones and dominions, the confederates of letters and religion. Let us go from the engine-room of the manufactory into the cabinet of the sovereign, upon whose single will the peace of the world depends; at whose bidding armies go forth to change the fate of countries, and the condition of millions. Life and death, liberty and slavery, fortune and ruin, appear to the outward eye as the messengers of his court; as if he could say to one, Go, and to another, Come, and they would obey. No lover of the race can behold power like this, vast in its range and apparently resistless in its course, without uneasiness;

and no disciple of the gospel can think of such a capacity for good or evil without the profoundest concern.

But there is a power transcending the sway of monarchs. Visit the great presses of the world, the fountains of knowledge, inspiration, and action; and from the headwaters of publication, follow the countless streams of literature as they spread themselves over and permeate the masses, poisoning or healing, raising or depressing, soothing or agitating, blessing or cursing, millions of souls. Here is power which has no assignable limit. It knows neither interruption nor abatement. It governs men through their will and passions, it rules their convictions and prejudices, it determines their path and their end, it is able to kill the soul as well as the body, and to send both into hell!

Now all the power represented by the one or two examples we have adduced, is in the hand of Christ; has been so from the time when He uttered the text on the Galilean Mount. He does not share the use of it with man. He is the head and source of it, the depositary and distributor; promoting, restraining, shaping, and absolutely controlling every species of power which we can conceive to exist in commerce, in government, in literature, in good and in evil. He is master of evil; the guilt of its malignity and uncleanness He reserves for the head of its inventors and agents; the power it possesses He appropriates and turns to his own account. He allows no kind of *force* to escape Him. For the humiliation of those who intend it as a weapon against Himself, He makes it an instrument to promote His own victory. The power of error, the power of scepticism, the power of superstition, the power of iniquity, do not run over the world lawless; they have, with the energy of everything that has activity, been given unto Jesus. We only see them corrupting, subverting, and destroying: we see the truth struggling against them, with a few followers, limited means, and disadvantageous ground. *The kings of the earth still set themselves, and the rulers take counsel together;* money, talent, wit, and rank, are still against us. Judas is still bartering his Master for silver; Simon Magus is still offering silver for ecclesiastical preferment; Ananias and Sapphira are still corrupting their dedication with a lie; and Demas is about to lose Christ and his soul for the love of the world. Looking at the amount and endless variety of adverse power in the world and in the church, we might well be depressed if we saw with no other eyes than our own; but watching with the eyes which God has planted within us, the spiritual sight reverses every testimony of the outward sense. We see all power acting for Christ. We see Him the sovereign of every cabinet, making peace and permitting war: kings may administer, but He reigns; princes may issue edicts, but He decrees justice: we see His purpose underlying the ambition of the great, the craftiness of the wise, and the resistance of the hostile; we see that all agents and events perform an office for heaven; every movement among men has a double application; it has its natural result answering to the experience of men, and at the same time it invisibly ministers to a higher end, executing the behests of God. Laying hold of this principle, we can look upon the struggling faith of Christianity with calmness; we see a friend in every foe, a help in every obstacle, a virtual co-operation in every assault; for all the power of that which is directed against us, is given to Christ, and He devotes it to the service of His people.

The same observations will apply to power not perceptible by us, but which affects us as closely as more tangible influences. All power "in heaven" is given unto Me. The powers of the invisible world whether they be thrones or dominions, whether they be instruments or occurrences, "these all wait upon him." It must be a source of great comfort and triumph to the people of God to learn that the invisible world which they know so imperfectly and dread so much, is as absolutely at the feet of their Lord as their own habitation. As an invisible Hand once fashioned and peopled this earth, so invisible hands have been engaged upon it ever since. To some of these we must attribute all the sorrow and misery our race has ever known. They have worked us from the beginning nothing but woe; and they are as busy and as malicious as ever. The power of wicked spirits can be imagined when it is known that they assume deceptive shapes, contrive deceptive circumstances, and whisper deceptive words, with an infinite diversity of imposture. No wonder that man is *led captive by the devil at his will.* The Prince and Power of the air exercises an apparent sway over the largest portions of our race. He is the incarnation of every false religion, the instigator of every wicked design, the author of every evil work; the first, the mightiest, and the last enemy of man; but Jesus came into the world to destroy his works, to translate souls from his power, and to bring his reign to an end. And this boastful King of darkness, this earliest apostate, usurper, and liar, has been compelled to surrender his realm to Christ: he is giving up his captives, retreating from his strongholds, and his own weapons are turned against himself.

But if we have enemies in the invisible world, we have friends also. If there are hands that do us wrong, there are hands diligently and lovingly engaged in ministering good to us. If there are spirits who rejoice in iniquity, there are more who *rejoice over one sinner that repenteth;* an innumerable company of angels, whose friendly legions are consecrated to the service and salvation of our race. All power is thus given unto Jesus, material, intellectual, circumstantial, angelical, infernal; He has received it for the benefit of His people and for the triumph of His cause. The Father hath given Him to be head over all things to the church which is His body. Daniel saw the august ceremony of the coronation, when the Father set His kingly offspring upon the holy hill: "I saw in the night visions, and, behold, one like the Son of man came with the clouds of heaven, and came to the Ancient of days, and they brought him near before him. And there was given him dominion, and glory, and a kingdom, that all people, nations, and languages should serve him : his dominion is an everlasting dominion which shall not pass away, and his kingdom that which shall not be destroyed."

We have here " the glorification of the Son by the Father." *All power is given unto Me :* " given by the Father in the fulfilment of the eternal covenant, in the Unity of the Holy Spirit."* The Father covenanted to open the kingdom of heaven to the human race upon the completion of the sufferings and sacrifice of the Divine Person who gave Himself to be a ransom for us. In His essential nature as the second person of the ever-blessed Trinity, all power was His from the beginning. But when He undertook to save man, not by prerogative, but in accordance with the judicial claims of His government, He assumed a position in which He was divested, as it were, of His omnipotence, His glory and His sovereignty; He became a man, to whom these attributes do not belong; He had the reputation of guilt, to which nothing belongs but the inheritance of pain and the infamy of execution. He had to win back by labour and expiration what we had lost. The cost at which it was possible for us to regain heaven was the

* *Vide* Alford's note on the text.

loss of His reputation; for He was numbered among transgressors and He bore the sin and shame of many: then followed the enforcement of suffering, the shedding of blood, and the awful violence and stroke of death. He had to endure all this; not as a man for his own sin, suffering the loss of an eye for an eye, and a tooth for a tooth; but as a world's victim. The sins of all ages and all races, the aggregate of the iniquity of all hearts, the crimes of all lives that ever did or ever shall deprave the nature of man were laid upon His soul. He answered for all, bled and expired for all, and the incense of the sacrifice went up, and God smelled a sweet savour, received His anointed back from the dead, and made Him the federal Head of a new race; placed the second Adam in a second paradise, and began for Him the creation of a new heaven and a new earth. Christ therefore received all power, as the second Father of our race, to bring His sons to glory. Having obtained the kingdom, He was invested with power to take possession of it, to draw all men unto Himself, to separate them from their errors, to pardon and wash them from their sins, to put His own glory upon their nature, and to deliver them absolutely from all their enemies.

This is the sphere and mission of His

power; and the gospel is its appointed instrument, being the power of God unto salvation unto every one that believeth, and the savour of death to every one that opposeth it. . All power is given unto Me to convert the world, Go ye therefore, and make Christians of all nations: lo, I am with you alway, even unto the end of the world. This, brethren, is the authority with which we go forth against the idolatries and the profoundly hostile mind of India; and this authority is the pledge of our success. We have on our side all power in heaven and in earth. We have felt it in our own conversion; we have seen its displays in our assemblies, bending the strong will, breaking the hard heart, arresting the torrent of passion, expelling a very legion-power of satanic influence, and making the fiercest adversary sit at the feet of Jesus, clothed, and in his right mind: we have seen it move on the individual spirit and on the collected mass; and sinners have fallen before it as grass is levelled by the mower's scythe. Need I revert to the examples that distant churches are witnessing of the power of Jesus? Perhaps in no former revival did the work of God ever assume such an aspect of power. It was preceded by no extraordinary means. No providential catastrophe, no ministerial eloquence, no officious but well-meant contrivances to awaken excitement; to none of these can be attributed that wonderful religious commotion which is now doing marvels in America and in Ireland. The power as it listeth has crept quietly on; men have not known whence it cometh or whither it goeth: from congregation to congregation, through the most unlikely neighbourhoods, where pride has been haughtiest, where vice has been boldest, where education, manners, and morals have been unknown,—the haunts of scepticism, the dens of crime, the shameful hiding places of poverty and misery,—the power has been passing like the breath of God when it renews the face of the earth. Men at first tried to arrest it; they doubted its origin, they circulated perverted reports of its operations, they speculated upon it in a spirit of philosophic banter, and many predicted the gravest mischiefs to society from its diffusion. But the power of Christ has held on its way, until its results have become too conspicuous for doubt, too serious for trifling, too active for indifference. The accession of multitudes to the church, the striking reduction of crime and social disturbance in those localities where the revival had prevailed, the marked diminution of public interest in sinful amusements, and the best symptoms of a healthy morality, have changed the public voice, and few will now venture to doubt *the finger of God;* men at least observe a respectful silence at what they do not understand, and they wait until God shall be His own interpreter.

Brethren, with these personal experiences, and with these facts ever multiplying, can we doubt that this country, too, shall fall before the advancing power of Jesus? I know the obstacles are mountainous. To change the convictions, the prejudices, and the habits of ages; to unbind races, that pride, interest, and a false faith, have united and consolidated; to bring them to the acceptance and open acknowledgment of the truth, and to make them bow the knee to Jesus, is not a work suitable to our capacity, and probably transcends the power of angels. We are not sent to attempt a work we cannot perform. He has commanded us to go and preach His gospel, and beseech men to be reconciled to Him; but when He adds, *Lo, I am with you,* He gives us the necessary condition of our success; for we do not regard this promise simply as a word of encouragement and good cheer. The presence of Christ is a part of our system. As the fact of His vicarious death is the foundation upon which we make the offer of forgiveness to men, so the power of His accompanying Spirit is the indispensable inspiration by which men are induced to accept that offer. Christ does not send us forth, and promise to help us in emergencies as if His power were reserved for seasons when our own power fails us. The work is His; the efficiency of all its operations is simply the result of a Divine power. Christ has condescended to employ us, and has promised that we shall share in the glory and spoils of victory: but the battle is the Lord's; His arm drives back the foe, and His banner waves over the surrendered citadel. Without me, said our Leader, ye can do nothing. Of some of our predecessors in this work and conflict, it is said, *They went forth and preached everywhere, the Lord working with them, and confirming the word, with signs following. Who then is Paul, and who is Apollos, but ministers by whom others believe, even as the Lord gives to every man. Therefore, my brethren, let us be steadfast, unmoveable, always abounding in the work of the Lord, forasmuch as ye know that your labour is not in vain in the Lord.*

SERMON VII.

ACTS xvi. 30.

"What must I do to be saved?"

I SHALL consider this text not as the cry of one startled by the light of truth, but as the question of a thoughtful person in some doubt as to the precise state of mind in which it would be *safe to die*. We are all drawing near death. Some are probably very near: and I shall take it for granted that all of us believe that the instant we cease to exist on earth we dwell in heaven or in hell. We may not be able vividly to conceive the fact; but it is nevertheless as true as anything we believe, that were all of us to die this moment, each one would be rejoicing or wailing the next; and our fate, whichever it might be, would not follow from any name we had assumed, from any rank we had held, from any profession we had made, but from the particular condition of our mind at the moment of death. We have no reason to suppose that any former experience will avail us in our last hour, supposing the safe state exist not then. Neither have we ground for thinking that we can be in a state between danger and safety, which God will hasten to the required crisis at the last moment. If God will hasten such a crisis, then is this state safe at any time. We are sure of heaven or sure of hell at any moment; that is, if the Bible be true; and if it be not true with respect to this doctrine, how can we accept any of its revelations? If then we are not conscious of preparation for heaven, our eternal state rests upon a *perhaps;* and a perhaps so doubtful, that in worldly matters we should hesitate to entrust to it the value of a shilling! To commit to a mere peradventure the issue of an eternal condition is madness: it is not so called because the world cannot see the egregious delusion implied in the risk.

But now let us enquire, in the fear of God and with profound reverence for truth, what is that state in which it is just safe to die? To be just safe is to be saved, using this word in its lowest sense; for gospel salvation comprehends with merely negative deliverance from hell, all the glorious experiences and capacities of the heavenly state. What shall I do to be just safe from the punishment of the wicked when I die? Consider Paul's reply, *Believe on the Lord Jesus Christ, and thou shalt be saved.* Consider also another passage which affirms that unless a man thus believe he shall not be saved, *He that believeth not the Son shall not see life, but the wrath of God abideth on him.* Whatever believing on Christ means, you must allow that unless our mind be in this state of believing we are not, I will not say justified and made holy, but *safe*. Take another verse, some of our Saviour's last words, *He that believeth not shall be damned.* We may differ on the nature of believing, on degrees of believing, on the results of believing, whether they are remote or immediate; but if we accept the plainest declarations of scripture, we shall not question the absolute necessity of faith in Christ in order to be just *safe*.

But we can make our ground narrower still, without meeting a single objection or explaining any theological term. Believing in Christ must express more than the hearing about Christ; to listen to a sermon on the Lord Jesus, to be familiar with the facts of the gospel narrative, to understand generally the nature of the Christian sacraments, may really mean no more than the listless reception of indifferent truth. I need not spend a moment to convince you that to be thus a hearer of the word, and to receive historical information about the Saviour, do not necessarily include believing on Him; and even though this knowledge remain with you for many years, and be expanded and refreshed from time to time by stated church-services, it does not therefore become *mixed with faith*. If any one of us were to die having gone no further than this, he would inevitably be damned: I say *inevitably*, because He who is the truth has clearly and repeatedly affirmed it. What that dread word means I know not; but to imagine it to be a light word, or a politic word inserted to frighten us—to suppose it to be any other than a word of terrible import, would be a levity which the most careless would hesitate to indulge. And yet if one of you were near death, and I knew that the amount of his preparation for eternity did not exceed the knowledge above described; in short, that he did not believe in Christ, and I were to see him die in that state, I could not so brave the restraints of courtesy as to declare that that soul was lost. I should be marked as a man without charity, without common Christian feeling: nay, I should not myself quickly believe that he who had so departed was in misery. My doctrine would avow it: but my ignorant and too sensuous nature would hope against it; while the habitual opinions of society, and the Christian ritual of interment, would deny it. These and other circumstances unite to disarm the fear of hell. Nevertheless, while we are trying to persuade ourselves that, in one of those tremendous last moments, God snatched that soul from the burning, it is, without doubt, perishing in the fire that will never be quenched; for *he that believeth not shall be damned.* Christian courtesy deals cruelly with souls, when it makes the punishment of the wicked a myth—the idle legend of a credulous age!

Hitherto we have asserted what no believer in the Bible can safely contradict. Let us yet narrow the ground a little: we have shewn that the hearing of Christ and the knowledge we may gather from sermons and books do not necessarily imply faith; a man may experience them without believing. It is, I think, also clear that to have faith in Christ means much more than to *think favourably of Him.* You would hardly substitute, He that admireth, for, He that believeth. If you study the events of Christ's life, you must admire. If innocence and humanity, self-sacrificing devotion to the happiness of others, and the largest and most fruitful philanthropy, can command reverence, it is impossible to read

H

the gospels and not adore. It is also difficult for an intelligent person to look at the Christian church—to examine her aims, to compute her results upon the world, the impressive helps and sanctions she lends to truth and goodness, and the restraints she imposes upon the ungodly, without the deepest admiration. Here is applause for Christ and for the church; but will a man dying in this state of mind be safe? He approves of Christianity, he praises Christian institutions; he knows the more popular doctrines of religion, highly commends the language in which they are stated, and the grand ideas they display; and, in the sense of having no objection to any of them, he admits them all. This is going a considerable way, even to positive approbation. A person so impressed would be attracted to religious assemblies; the habit of attending them would insensibly grow into a sort of identity with those who had really believed; and, without closely examining his mind, he might suppose that this mental, this tasteful acceptance of Christianity is the same in kind with that personal belief in Christ which we insist on as the sole condition of *safety*. He would hence regard himself as one of the lowest class of believers, and presume that, if he continued his attentions to religion, attentions gradually advancing him to a fellowship with the church, a pitiful and long-suffering God would not, in the last moment, *quench the smoking flax*. That which would assist this inference into a kind of hope would be the fact that the language in which he expressed his *opinions* would much resemble the style in which true believers recite their *experience;* confession of sin, the conflicts of unbelief, the assaults of temptation, anxious doubts of forgiveness, and similar marks and descriptions of the *new life*, would seem to accord with his state in common with that of the *safe* Christian.

But in all this we have seen no belief in Christ at all. To say nothing of *degrees* of faith and assurance, faith has not *begun!* This is no mere notion, but a fact which all who credit the scriptures must admit. A man may go to the length of hearing about Christ, approving of Christian doctrine, mingling with Christian believers, speaking a Christian language, and supporting a Christian cause, without attaining the lowest degree of safety: if a man go no further, and die within the limit of these associations, die though he may in the bosom of the visible church, esteemed by the minister, beloved by God's people, and admired by all for his consistency and sincerity, he will, in spite of all, *be cast into outer darkness, where there is weeping and wailing and gnashing of teeth.* He may be a preacher of the gospel, or a member of a Christian family: no *position* will save him. You may have a difficulty in realizing this; there may be a social impropriety in your speaking on this issue with confidence of any particular individual; but oh! doubt it not! for the safety of your immortal souls, doubt it not! How many at this moment are lifting up their eyes in personal torment, whose remains we interred under the formula of "a sure and certain hope!" We think of them without disturbance, because memory parted with them at the grave's mouth. It is unnatural to entertain hard thoughts of the *dead;* but let the living fear. Let us be severe and exact to ourselves, if we are charitable to others. It is a harrowing meditation, to imagine that some of those whom we once esteemed or loved for their wisdom, affection, and integrity, should now be writhing under the anguish of the curse of God! There are some who will whisper, "This is a hard saying, who can hear it?" Be not hasty to take offence, before you have seen the ground upon which the doctrine rests.

Believe on the Lord Jesus Christ, and thou

shalt be saved. This is uniformly stated to be the ground of salvation. It is asserted in various ways, but the principal term is the same. I need not remind you that the reason why Jesus is set forth as the object of our belief or trust, is the fact of His having died for our sins. When He expired on the cross He became a propitiation. We sometimes call this an appeasing of the Father, or a reconciling to Him; the meaning is, that Christ averted or turned aside the penalty to which sin had made us liable, by Himself suffering it. Now from whom is that punishment turned aside? From those "who have faith in his blood." In other words, that man is safe who believes that in suffering death, Jesus was his effectual substitute, annulling the requirement of his own death. Does not this plan commend itself to your sense of what is becoming and just? Is it unfair that God should restrict salvation to those who accept the Saviour? But you will ask,—Did not the individual whom you just now left without hope so accept the Saviour when he admired Him, approved His doctrines, and joined His people? Not so: for if sin be personal, that is, if each be accountable for his own sins, the belief that gives us a claim to the propitiation must be personal too. If every one of us must render an account of himself to God, it follows that the death of Christ has not procured an amnesty or general pardon for all the guilty; but for those only who accept that death as an atonement. Now, it is not possible for you to perform this act of faith without making the death of Jesus an object of particular attention. There must be a strong feeling of its necessity; a motive to urge the mind to cleave to it as a refuge. There must be a coming out from cloudy generalities, as, that the character of Christ is lovely, that Christ died for sinners, that the Christian cause is worth supporting, and that everything in the Bible is true. Two facts must hold the attention: first—I am a sinner deserving everlasting misery, in myself without help and without hope; if I die in this state I shall be lost. Secondly—deliverance is offered me; Jesus the Son of God died in my stead: it is affirmed that if I accept Him as an atonement, I shall be saved. Here is a hiding-place for me; is it worthy my trust? Does it appear equal to the security it engages to provide? Is there no other way? If, giving anxious and exclusive attention to Christ, I am led to receive Him as my Saviour, the sacrifice once offered for my sins, then, and not until then, I am safe.

If in this discussion I avoid the prescribed phrases of theology, it is to separate from the things they signify the occasionally distracting influence of words of technical usage. Now, if you are conscious of having thus closed with the gospel offer, of having accepted Jesus for yourself, you may be safe: if you have not thus received Him, then, dying in this state, I will not say the risk, but the certainty of damnation is upon you. I will not ask whether you are conscious of pardon, whether you have the witness of the Spirit, what degree of assurance you have. I will not perplex your examination of this one act of recumbency upon Jesus, by insisting now upon this or that result; but I inquire, in the fear of God, of every one present, whether in any period of his life that transaction of belief, for his own salvation, in the atoning death of Jesus was ever effected? I insist not upon accuracy of moment or of place in stating the change, but the act is so important, and is attended in its various efforts by so much anxiety and excitement, that every one who has made it *must be conscious that he has made it*. This receiving of Christ procures for us the *lowest degree of safety:* and those who do not believe that this distinct experience was ever their own, are now on the margin of everlasting death. I feel a reluctance in admitting so much, but plain duty bids me declare that such persons may at any time awake in the unquenchable fire. God is no respecter of persons, situations, or gifts: He is not swayed by that local charity, pity, and respect, which bribe our judgment, and which, in religious opinion, are as erroneous as they are amiable. He speaks and acts from the centre of universal harmony: He has exhibited a propitiation for sin, and decreed that it shall benefit those only who personally and wholly accept it.

My dear hearers, I have delivered what I sincerely believe to be the truth, and I will not apologize for using great plainness of speech. I only wish I could have spoken with the force and earnestness which such a subject ought to inspire. May God impress it upon your hearts! especially upon the consciences of those who have done everything for Christianity but believe in Christ; who have received everything from Christianity but a new heart; who are in the melancholy condition of lacking nothing but the one thing needful! May His Spirit subdue prejudice, awaken apathy, dispel error, and shed a light upon the danger of those who are not prepared to die, that shall compel them to cry out, "What must I do to be saved?"

SERMON VIII.

2 Tim. ii. 13.

"If we believe not, yet he abideth faithful: he cannot deny himself."

THESE words may be understood as relating to something which God has propounded to man, or to something which He has appointed for man. They imply the possibility of God's revelation being discredited, or His decrees resisted, and affirm that no conduct of ours, under any circumstance, can affect His constancy. He has revealed His gospel for our acceptance and salvation; He has decreed certain providential arrangements for our concurrence and benefit: if we assent to His proposals, we must take them as they are; for the terms upon which they have been made are unalterable. *If we believe not, yet He abideth faithful.* There are three classes of persons to whom this passage may be applied.

1. *The sceptic*, or he who believes not for want of evidence. The lesson conveyed to him is this, God has not provided against

every doubt. He has not revealed His will so clearly as to compel conviction. Belief is invited, and even courted; and when rendered is vindicated and rewarded: but it is not made necessary by a constitutional bias for religion, or by evidence which it would be absurd to question. And yet this is a kind of testimony which many inquirers demand of the Christian religion. They object that so grave a subject as a revelation from God, a revelation which proposes to lead the soul out of darkness and prepare it for immortality, should admit of suspicion; they maintain that it ought to be impossible for any mind, however sceptically disposed, to doubt principles, on the admission or rejection of which depend such vast results as eternal happiness and eternal woe. They add, moreover, with much apparent reason, that men's susceptibilities of belief are as diverse as their physical varieties. Some assent at once to what is simply announced; they ask for no chain of evidence, for they have neither the power nor the patience to follow you through separate links of reasoning. Others have minds quick to perceive difficulties and apt to suggest them; they have been in the habit of grappling with hard questions, and use has made their powers keen in argument and expert in debate.

Many have been unfortunate in their education. They imbibed sceptical notions before they understood them; were taught from their youth to discredit the New Testament; and they find it impossible to believe. Now, say our objectors, the Christian religion ought to prove itself divine with equal force to every class of understanding.

Assuming that God is the author of Christianity, is it likely either that the revelation itself, or the terms upon which its benefits are offered, or the manner of making it known, would so agree with our notions as to preclude objection? Unquestionably not: for nature herself has not escaped criticism, and even providence has been arraigned to answer for measures which man's ignorance has pronounced erring or unjust. Hence it cannot be supposed that religion, to which men's prejudices are peculiarly hostile, should be accepted without scruple. But did we ever know or hear of a sincere inquirer into the evidences of the Christian faith driven back in hopeless scepticism? Sceptics there are; some of them are apparently settling into atheism, others are reposing in deism, and many are wandering restless through the chaos of speculation. But these unhappy persons are not the victims of a *doubtful religion;* they stumble over no immoveable obstacles: they simply disdain the terms on which the seeker is promised success. And those terms are not dissimilar to the conditions exacted by nearly every province of knowledge. They are honesty, humility, and earnestness. Is it too much that God should expect men to be candid, modest, and anxious, in their search after truth and immortality? The Bible has an argument for every man. God who knows what is in man has deemed it sufficient for conviction. The learned require one kind of proof, the ignorant need another; and the infinite variety of mind in the human family arising from epoch, race, and education, must be met by a corresponding versatility of treatment. This diversity of proof has been furnished, and so triumphantly does it defend Christianity, that of the thousands who believe not, there are few, very few, who even profess to reject it because its demonstrations are not conclusive.

God has revealed His will for the faith of man: He has supported it by appropriate and ample evidence; by prophecy, by miracles, and by that inward consciousness which, if honestly questioned, answers to and corroborates all testimony. He has overlooked no possible circumstance in which man can be placed. All His requirements are within the ability of the human mind; and hence with perfect justice He has affixed the heaviest penalties to scepticism,—" He that believeth not shall be damned." To that word God will be faithful; it is a law as uniform in its operations as the order of the universe. Were any exception made, or any clause introduced to qualify the edict, God would deny Himself. You may imagine that in your case, at least, the rule may be relaxed, and that pity will be shown to an unbelief so helpless as yours; but this would be as foolish as to suppose that nature would reverse her laws to save that man from destruction who, without intending it, should fall over a precipice. In both instances man might find an excuse, but God's law would be inexorable. In both instances, HE *abideth faithful; He cannot deny Himself.*

2. *The careless unbeliever.* We have here to do with a state of mind nearly opposite to scepticism. At first sight the doctrine that God will concede nothing to wilful neglect seems too obvious for exposition. But if we connect it with human nature, we shall see that while men assent readily to a broad principle of morality, each person is disposed to shun its application to himself. A man will denounce lying, yet justify an equivocation of

his own; another will condemn gambling; but being a man of principle, will excuse an occasional game of chance for his own recreation. Every vice will thus find its apologist; especially those that lie in the more fascinating walks of sin, or such as appear to befriend a particular interest or passion. This disposition to evade the truth is very apparent when we are summoned to hear a message from God. When we tell you that God commands you to repent and believe in His Son, you answer that nothing can be more reasonable; when we add that unless you believe, you will be lost, you rejoin that nothing can be more just; when we insist that the word of the eternal is unchangeable, that He has said with regard to threatenings and promises, "I the Lord change not," you acknowledge that nothing can be more true; and yet, while you quickly accept these declarations, each person holds back from the duty they involve. Every one imagines that in *his* case the precept is not urgent, the threatening does not apply; there is something *he* has done, or that he intends to do, or that it is impossible he should do, that disarms the truth of its force when applied to himself. Perhaps one endeavours to believe that there never was a case exactly parallel with his own, in which a religious life has met with difficulties absolutely insuperable. On this presumption he builds a hope that our heavenly and all-loving Father has left a margin in His gracious plan to meet cases that fall out of the ordinary course of life. Perhaps another defers his duty; he promises to consider these things more seriously hereafter, and to obtain the Redeemer's salvation before he dies; assuming that no delay is so excusable as his, and no promise more sincerely made or more likely to be fulfilled.

We may comprehend within this section of unbelievers a very large number who cannot be said to hold any opinion on religion; they are satisfied with a general knowledge of the Bible and church; but they avoid details, and consider it both discreet and meritorious to belong to that class who *profess* nothing. Thus they save themselves from the common sins of insincerity and hypocrisy; they are neutral, but not false. Multitudes of respectable people agree with them, and they hope it will be well with all such at last.

From these instances of self-defence against the application of God's truth, it is clear that while nothing is easier to be proved, nothing is harder to enforce than the proposition that God will accommodate no law to meet what we may choose to call exceptional circumstances. The character of the Almighty forbids us to imagine that He will yield to the apologies of the sinner. He does not act from fugitive impressions, but from the dictates of His understanding; an understanding that encompasses all knowledge—a knowledge of possible things, and of real things. This omniscience is the rule of that providence which God exercises over the works of His hand. He who created the universe and preserves it, must necessarily and perfectly understand it; as the moral governor of the world and the dispenser of rewards and punishments, He must know the moral character of His subjects. With this knowledge He framed the gospel. He had the human race before Him, its divisions, its varieties, its successive generations, its unfolding capabilities, its possible vicissitudes; no phase of character, single or collective, escaped Him. Of the countless millions that passed under this omniscient survey, not one individual was lost. You were there, and I, and as we stood before His future-piercing eye, with our peculiarities, our difficulties, and our apologies, He wrote down with the deliberation of eternity, " He that believeth not shall be damned."

Can I, a poor worm among the millions for whom He then legislated, imagine that that eternal law can be reversed for me? That the mind that planned and presides over all things will bend its mighty decrees to conciliate me? That He will consult my fanciful and unmeaning wishes, and forget the honor of his truth? That though He has said from eternity, if I believe not in His Son I shall be lost, I shall *not* be lost even though I do *not* believe? That in the government of nature, of providence, and of grace, He will abide faithful to His word, except when that word applies to *me?* That for my sake He will vacillate, and equivocate, and deny Himself? I will not say that the supposition is irrational,—though if it belonged to ordinary questions we might dismiss it with a more contemptuous epithet; but it is a signal instance of the deluding power of the heart which, *deceitful above all things*, ensnares the most wary and vigilant. Reason, experience, conscience, all become the victims of its magical duplicity. That a man, who, in other respects, is discreet and of a sound judgment, cautious in his ventures and reasonable in his expectations, should, in regard to the salvation of his soul, be cheated by an obvious and silly imposition, an imposition which cannot hide itself from the dullest sense! O brethren, give as much reflection to this matter as you bestow upon your worldly affairs, and you will see that it is as impossible for you who have not forsaken sin and accepted Christ, to go to heaven, as it is for God to lie. Nor is this an arbitrary decree. The law which sends an unbeliever to hell is not at variance with the law which admits the believer to heaven. It is the law of affinities. We contain within ourselves our hereafter, and take our eternal state with us. He who has lived without God in this world, lives on without God in the next. Were God to admit the unbeliever to heaven there could be no heaven there for him. I appeal to *you* who are not reconciled to the Father,—who never draw near to the throne of grace, who have no relish for spiritual conversation, who prefer worldly people, worldly topics, worldly books, and worldly maxims, to the society and manners of the godly,—I appeal to *you* whether if God were to open for you the kingdom of heaven, you would find there a society and an employment congenial to your taste? You would be a stranger in a strange land! Your sins unpardoned, the remembrance of having doubted the word of God, and rejected Christ, and quenched the Spirit, would inflict the sharpest anguish of hell! In the midst of heaven's beatitudes, of songs in which you could not join, employments with which you could not sympathize, revelations which you could not appreciate, pleasures which you could not taste, a God whom you could not call Father, a Christ whom you could not call Brother, and angels and saints whom you could not call companions, under the very shadow of the tree of life, you would be a lost soul, uttering the woe of an inseparable doom,

> Me miserable! Which way shall I fly,
> Infinite wrath, and infinite despair?
> Which way I fly is hell; myself am hell!

3. *The Christian.* In applying the text to the people of God, the words will refer to the terms of a covenant, rather than to the conditions of belief. We *have* believed: faith has brought us into fellowship with Christ, a fellowship maintained by the fulfilment of promises on both sides. Both have engaged to be faithful; but whatever becomes of *our troth*, Christ will never deny His. "If we believe not, He abideth faithful." The words that go before the text convey a very

impressive warning. "If we deny him, He also will deny us." But while they foretell an awful doom for the apostate, they give good cheer to timid and self-distrusting disciples, assuring them that those involuntary moods of feeling in themselves, the depressing infirmities of piety, to which we often ascribe the importance of more serious changes, affect not the stedfastness of the Divine love. If *we* tremble in the presence of an adversary, or at the prospect of suffering, if at any time we allow our hope and fear to change with the shifting colors of the outer world, by which we are so often made to rejoice or sorrow at the wrong season, Christ abideth the unchangeable Lord, ruling the vicissitudes that alarm or gladden us, and promoting the consummation we long for by the obstacles that discourage us, and by the enemies we fear. Let us remember, moreover, that these miserable weaknesses of faith, so unworthy the love we profess, and so base when contrasted with the unalterable fidelity of Jesus, awaken in Him no displeasure; they touch the pity of His heart—not simply the pity of the strong for the weak, which has often a species of derision underlying it, but the nearer sympathy of One who is in a certain sense answerable for what He pities; the profoundly respectful tenderness of the FIRST-BORN for His brethren. Let us cleave to our Brother in love and in trust, and find a Sabbath for our restless spirits in the cleft of *a Rock that is higher than we.*

SERMON IX.

HEBREWS vii. 25.

"*Wherefore He is able also to save them to the uttermost that come unto God by Him, seeing He ever liveth to make intercession for them.*"

THIS verse was written to encourage the penitent sinner, to revive the faith of the doubtful, and the courage of the timid. I pray that the Holy Spirit may open its meaning to our hearts, that each one of us may be moved to accept it for himself!

The text gives us an account of a *priest;* of one by whose assistance we approach our holy Creator, and who ever liveth to speak for us before God. A priest is a sacrificer—one who kills a victim. The custom of shedding the blood of animals in connection with the worship of God began, as you are aware, in the earliest ages of the world: priesthood began with it. Some one was appointed to take the life of the animal selected for sacrifice, to present its blood to God, and to offer for himself and fellow-worshippers an intercessory prayer. This man was called the sacrificer, or priest. You are aware that in patriarchal days, the days that went before the founding of the Jewish nation, there were no religious institutions, no temples, no united congregations; but every pious family was a little church, and the father of the household was the priest. In the morning and evening he called together his wife, children, servants, and any stranger or neighbour who happened to be within his gates; and before them all he slew the victim or presented the fruits, and prayed for them all, not forgeting the absent. We learn so much from the history of Noah, Abraham, and Job. We may suppose that the family and domestics of these holy fathers were no less the objects of their solicitude, than the flocks and herds that composed their wealth. The patriarchal rule was both wise and necessary; for the first families of men were, as you might suppose, extremely rude: there were no books, and no employments beyond the simple cares and the unimportant enterprizes of a shepherd's life: while, on the other hand, the wickedness of these ancient tribes was quite equal to their opportunities. The children and servants of a house received their moral lessons from the father and master, and they laid their religious anxieties upon him: he confessed their sins, made atonement for them, and committed them at all seasons into the hands of God; he was their ambassador to God, their intercessor, their mediator. I need scarcely remind you that this state of things was changed when Abraham's family became a nation. Then the priesthood, instead of being represented in every house, was vested in one tribe, and consisted of several orders, such as the high-priest, priests, and Levites : but priesthood, whatever shape it assumes—whether Patriarchal, Levitical, or Christian, *is the indispensable law of our intercourse with God.* There must be a sacrifice and the shedding of blood; there must be a person approved and called of God to offer that atonement, and to procure the acceptance of our devotions and religious service. There may be a change in the priesthood, but priesthood itself must continue while God retains His holiness and man his sin. There must be sacrifice to the end of the world, and the interposition of a third party to stand for us in the presence of God.

In the text the writer of this epistle speaks of the priest whom God has ordained for *us*. As the old shepherd-priests were supplanted by the Levitical ministers, so these in their turn were put aside for another order of priesthood, resembling in its simplicity and in its freedom from ritual encumbrance, the old form of Abraham and Melchisedec. This is the unchangeable priesthood of Jesus Christ, fore-ordained in the beginning, and of which the earlier forms were types, preliminary institutions, that had no significancy or benedictory virtue, but in so far as they pointed to the last and greater order. When Abraham slew his victim, it was the priesthood of Christ that made that victim acceptable; when Aaron entered the tabernacle made with hands, and sprinkled blood upon the holiest, his memorial went up before God a sweet savour, because his faith discerned the "greater and more perfect tabernacle, not of this building," and rested upon the Lamb that was slain from the foundation of the world. The priesthood of Christ does not so much supplant other orders, as it fulfils them. Now one of the most important subjects which a religious man can inquire into is the priesthood under which he lives. And this is the topic before us. We are not going to discuss an order of things that has passed away, nor are we going to expatiate on the merits of any party hierarchy of the present time; but we shall endeavour to set before you your own priest, to recall the service He has done for you, and the infinite benefits you derive, or may derive, from His office. Let us comprise these considerations within the two statements of the text, "He ever liveth to make intercession for us," and, by the prerogative of this office, " He is able to save to the uttermost all that come unto God by Him."

"He ever liveth to make intercession for us." He ever liveth to go between the Father and us, to speak, to mediate, between God and man. The high priest's office on the great day of expiation will give us a vivid impression of the gracious work of Christ. Imagine the people of Israel assembled on that day as near the tabernacle as they dared to approach. They are come to confess a long list of crimes and to entreat for mercy. One of themselves is appointed to plead for them. His first act in this work of intercession is to kill,—to take life: "the blood of bulls and of goats" flows copiously; and collecting what he has shed into a vessel, the holy man lifts the veil, passes with the blood into the most holy place, and advancing with trembling steps to the mercy-seat, he stands in the glorious presence of Jehovah. Here he represents two things, life forfeited, and life taken, the sinner and the victim. *Wilt Thou accept this, for this?* life taken for life forfeited? And the answer is flashed forth from between the cherubim in rays of mercy, lighting up the face of the holy man, who returns to his condemned brethren outside, to announce that the blood has prevailed and that the sinner may go free! So Christ, our High Priest, offered Himself without spot; submitted to be bound and slain as an unblemished lamb reared for the altar; and having poured out His blood, He has, as it were, taken it into the holy of holies, into the presence of God; and there He stands interceding for us whom He has left outside, guilty, trembling in the prospect of wrath to come, but awaiting the result of His prayer. "Father! justly art Thou angry with those who have resisted Thy authority, taken arms against Thee, and insulted Thy holiness by a depraved life. Their least crime merits the doom of banishment from Thy presence: they have nothing to say in extenuation of their sin, they have nothing to offer as the price of their redemption, they have nothing to promise as an amendment of their condition. Thy law has condemned them to die; they confess the sentence just, and abide the stroke of Thy vengeance. Father! I loved them, and went down amongst them; and became poor, and suffering, and miserable, and naked, for their sake; and when I saw Thy sword pursuing them, I cried, O sword, awake against Me, the Lord's shepherd, against the man that is the Lord's fellow: smite the shepherd, and let the sheep escape! And the sword turned and went through *Me;* it entered My heart, and behold here is the blood which it drew, and here are the wounds which it made: I bring them; I bring all in the stead of the sinner; place them against the liabilities of the sinner; My agony and bloody sweat, My cross and passion, My death, resurrection, and ascension; take them all, and give Me back the pardon of the sinner!"

> "The Father hears Him pray,
> His dear anointed one;
> He cannot turn away
> The presence of His Son.
> His Spirit answers to the blood,
> And man is reconciled to God."

Christ is thus in the presence of God for us, an appeasing victim, and a supplicating priest; the victim accepted, and the priest heard. It is not that Christ exhibits His atonement to the Father at *stated times:* He is *ever* before God. His own people will always find Him there, faithfully and affectionately conducting their cause; leaving nothing undone, nothing unsaid, nothing forgotten, which can in any way help their intercourse with God and their journey to glory. The penitent will always find Him there, anxious to promote a meeting between grace and guilt; helping the first efforts of repentance, directing the earnest yet distrustful prayer of the contrite spirit, and procuring and sending home to the disconsolate breast the message of pardon. The tried spirit will always find Him there, no stranger to trial Himself; and whatever be the temptation that presses; of the numberless and various evils that make this life a battle, whichever happens to imperil or hurt, He understands it, has Himself encountered it, and strengthens to bear, or lifts the burden upon His own shoulders; doing all this with a tenderness so mindful, with a love so new and rich in its unfoldings, that some of the very happiest hours of a Christian's life are the hours of affliction: but whatever be their texture, the good man perceives that his sufferings unite to improve his temper, establish his faith, correct his mistakes, purify his desires, and meeten his spirit for heaven. The child of God ever remembers a chastisement with thankfulness, *It is good for me that I have been afflicted.*

But there is another view in which the intercession of Christ may be regarded. It has an important influence upon our own prayers. Christ brings the "form of God" within the apprehension of the worshipper. We prostrate ourselves in prayer to ask for the Divine mercy, but how helpless we are! We feel acutely the evil we wish to have removed; but the Being we approach is an infinite Spirit, like nothing which we see, nothing which we have known: we hear of Him by the hearing of the ear—we assemble in our minds every object of thought, every image, that can help our conception of an eternal, omniscient, and immaculate Spirit, "upholding all things by the word of His power;" but this greatness oppresses us: if we are not overawed, we are stupefied, by it. We cannot realize the personal notice of the Infinite; and then occurs the thought of our own insignificance,—" Can *my* voice reach the ear of the Eternal? Can any prayer from my corrupt and infirm soul—so foolish, vain, ignorant, and unclean, attract the regard, or even the notice of the Holy One? Am I not conscious of a guilty life? Does not the remembrance of a thousand acts of rebellion rush in upon my soul like a flood, and extinguish prayer?" But suppose that, while I am thus contending with slavish fear, scepticism, and other powers of darkness, kneeling down, but not humble; uttering words of prayer but not praying; now disgusted with myself for being a hypocrite, now angry with revelation for not being so clear and straightforward as to make doubt impossible: suppose, I say, that during this struggle, a friend enters my closet. I relate to him what I feel; describe as nearly as I can the contradictory views and conflicting emotions which agitate me when I attempt to pray. He understands my case, tells me he has passed through the same difficulties; and as he solves my doubts and anticipates my objections, and disentangles my knotty opinions, I find that he knows more of me than I know of myself: and when he proposes that we kneel down together and approach the throne of God's majesty in company, his prayer seems to prepare the way for mine; and the thought of being in such circumstances with *another*, stronger, holier, and more deeply versed in the conflicts of mind than I am, restores a confidence not unlike that which a sinking man regains, when he leans upon the shoulder of a strong swimmer who has plunged into the tide to save him.

Now imagine that the friendly visitor who opens your closet door at the hour of prayer is *Christ*. He enters and finds you bowed down before God, trying to pray, but not able; He approaches, kneels with you, and whispers with great gentleness, " I am the way, and the truth, and the life; no man cometh unto the Father but by me." And not like an ordinary friend, this comforter and intercessor is as exactly conscious of your state of mind as you are; and not with wise counsels and soothing words only, but with spiritual influences and revelations does He assist the painful efforts of prayer: and more than all, He who kneels with you, as a fellow-suppliant, not only touches *you* with His human nature, but touches *God* with His divine; and that which one nature urges Him to ask, another nature enables Him to bestow: He has all the sympathy which man can have for man, and all the power which man can need from God! Are you perplexed with suspicions and dark controversies in prayer? He answers, " My thoughts are not your thoughts, neither are your ways my ways, saith the Lord. Commit your reasonings to me: be of good cheer, only believe." Are you distressed with a fear that one so guilty, so depraved, so penetrated with spiritual leprosy as you are, can never be made clean? He replies, " My blood cleanseth from all sin. I will sprinkle clean water upon you, and you shall be clean. If you can believe that I am what I declare Myself to be—the propitiation which God has accepted for you, and your all-prevailing advocate and helper in the divine presence, though your sins be as scarlet, they shall be white as snow, though they be red like crimson, they shall be as wool."

No, blessed be God! we do not approach Him alone. We come leaning on the arm of our almighty advocate, whose redeeming work and unchangeable office guarantee the success of our prayers, the victory of our conflicts, and the happiest issue of our probation; for, "He is able to save to the *uttermost;*" the best sense of which word is, to the *utmost of our need, entirely, in the highest degree.* We know not into what extremes of danger and distress we may be hurried; our future is an untried one; but this we know, we shall be saved to the *uttermost.* We know not the ingredients of the cup our Father is mixing for us; singular revolutions may be in store for us; times, places, events, may be ushered into the scene, to blast our earthly hopes, to strip us of our dearest fellowships, to take from under us our fondest supports: an adverse wind may be permitted to shake every

K

root and fibre that binds us to the earth, and to beat against each other the boughs and branches of our estate, until not one leaf be left to relieve the desolation; but let the fig-tree wither in its blossom, and fruit be denied to the vines; let the labor of the olive fail, and the fields yield no meat; let the flock be cut off from the fold, and let there be no herd in the stalls*—we shall be saved to the uttermost. But inward struggles may await us no less than outward changes. We have committed ourselves to Christ for life and for death. We may go on with a chequered experience like Bunyan's pilgrim; now climbing the hill Difficulty, now stumbling in the Valley of Humiliation, now fording the Slough of Despond, now battling with Giant Despair; now taking a view of the city from the Delectable Mountains, and anon groping our dark and perilous way through the Valley and Shadow of Death—until we are startled by the river that has neither bridge nor ferry. We will not think too curiously or anxiously of what may befall us there; whether we shall look wistfully down into its glassy depths and shrink at the cold touch of its margin waves, or whether we shall breast it manfully, like a

Hab. iii. 17.

ship going into harbour. We will leave the manner, as well as the time of our getting across to the Leader who has brought us with so signal a power through many dangers and will not desert us in the last. Be the passage rough or smooth, we shall make it, and, planting our foot on the opposite side, shout, *Saved to the uttermost!*

SERMON X.

ZECHARIAH ix. 17.

" How great is his goodness, and how great is his beauty!"

MAN, though he has lost a natural power to be good, retains the ability to perceive goodness, and the taste to admire it. These are some of the subordinate instruments of his restoration; for our conception of excellence, greatly surpassing our endeavours to recover it, is an image of virtue constantly before us, and excites us to efforts after goodness which, but for such a pattern, we should never attempt. But the imagination of virtue, though attractive enough to win our applause, is not sufficiently distinct to guide our imitation. He would never become a painter who should draw exclusively from the *beau ideal* of his fancy. He must spend his days over the canvas of other masters, and chain his observation down to what has been done, before he allows his genius to muse on what might be done. The works of another performer will teach him the rules of his art, educate his taste, and give a cheerful stimulus to his ambition. So in the study of moral excellence, we must have the model of a real character before us, and be instructed in the laws by which its beautiful proportions have been wrought, and learn how to make those initial efforts by which the imitator approaches it.

Such a model is Christianity's revelation of God; and herein it may be contrasted with other religions. The mythologies of Paganism are a variety of embodied ideas, such as justice, might, wisdom, and providence; worshipped under various types of power,—a hero, a beast, an element, &c. But in Christianity these scattered fragments of excellence are united into one perfect and matchless whole; they are the attributes of a living God—the Deity of the universe. Our text does not celebrate abstract qualities, but the known character of a Being who is attached to us by every natural and tender bond, and to whom we are indebted for our existence, and all its capacities and pleasures. Let us present Him to our minds in the character celebrated by the prophet, His goodness and His beauty.

His goodness is a moral attribute. His beauty is the harmonious effect of His whole character. He is beautiful because He is good.

His goodness is the spring of His own and of all beauty. Whatever be the true theory of beauty, whether we suppose we are made conscious of it by a distinct faculty, or whether it is a conformity to what is most usual, or whether it depends upon mental associations, He is the author of those pleasurable emotions which we derive from beauty. If we examine the objects that wake up feelings of this kind, we shall find that they have in them some element of *goodness*. A child is a beautiful object; but the ruddy colours and graces of childhood would not so sensibly gratify the eye, were they not blended with innocence and simplicity. I have often admired an English landscape, with its sloping hills spotted with cattle, the neat cottages that lie within the valley, the old church that " points with taper spire to heaven," the distant plough, and the brook that sings merrily by. All this, I have exclaimed, is beautiful; but on examining the pleasure that moved me, I have found it to arise, not from the physical features of the scene, but from the associations they suggested. They were images of plenty and contentment, of peace, piety, and simplicity; and were contrasted with the noise, fever, and guilt of a large city: and more than this, everything I saw, fields, houses, trees, children, spoke eloquently of God. The exclamation of the text was taken up and whispered from insect to insect, and from flower to flower, *How great is His goodness, and how great is His beauty!*

This thought makes nature altogether lovely. I would rather be a simple peasant who looks upon creation with the exulting thought that his Father made it all, than the philosopher whose investigations have not led him to God. He has learned the structure of nature and can give you the history of a plant, the genus of an animal, the revolution of a star. He can discourse learnedly of skill and fitness, of law and power; he can open cabinets of nature where wisdom has hidden her most curious relics; but if he see no goodness in all this, if there be not the glow of a holy worship in his heart, rising to the fountain of the various and beautiful creations around him, he may call himself a lover of nature, but nature rejects his suit; he may announce himself a believer in the eternal laws, but those very laws condemn him, and he is, as it were, outlawed from the sympathy and fellowship of creation. But the believer in the goodness of God, without science, finds a higher delight in his contemplation of nature than your mere man of problems and cyclopædias. He can account for nothing he beholds; he is no botanist, no natural philosopher, no astronomer; but the pious heart makes amends for the unlettered eye. He has learned the best science; that God has given him all things richly to enjoy; that light and air, colours and sounds, all that sustains and all that gratifies, are blessings which an infinite goodness has freely and generously bestowed, to lead those who enjoy them to Himself, the crown of all His gifts.

But when science unites with piety; when she follows her studies with the humility of an inquirer, instead of the authority of a dictator; when she submits to follow where she lacks both strength and knowledge to lead, she is a glorious witness for God. Science has been indefatigable in her labours and illustrious in her success. When she first appeared, atheism claimed her for a companion and an advocate; but she who was hired to curse, began, like Balaam, to bless the God of Israel. She took up a parable against the ignorance and absurdities of scepticism, against the heartless and destructive theories of infidelity; she demonstrated not only an original and pervading mind, that first contrived, and then wrought, and now sustains all things, but she proved by irresistible testimony that that

Being is good to all, that His tender mercy is over all His works. Wherever she detected skill, she found love: in cases where the benevolence of God was doubtful, where His doings appeared to manifest sternness, cruelty, or indifference, she explored the secret of the unwelcome phenomenon, and discovered a blessing in it. That which appeared dark and threatening, was secretly averting an evil or educing a good. She ascended to those glorious stars above us, and found nothing but goodness there; she dived into the lower deeps, and from their crowded archives fetched up records that tell of nothing but goodness there; she decomposed the elements, analysed their proportions, and determined their affinities, and she found innumerable proofs of goodness there. She pursued the history of the great and the small in creation, from the elephant down to the tiniest races of life, she gathered them together in classes like Noah, and like Adam, she gave them names: she knows their structure, their habits, their wants, and their supplies; and finds a most tender ministry, and a most perfect government over them all, for *He openeth His hand and satisfieth the desire of every living thing.* How great is His goodness, and how great is His beauty!

This is the song of creation. *Day unto day* chants it in all languages, and the still small voices of night melt into the music of the grand hymn which the morning stars composed in the beginning, when *all the sons of God shouted for joy.*

But the goodness which affects ourselves is the most touching and impressive. We are more qualified to admire its operations at home than its manifestations abroad. The goodness of a benefactor is admirable in the sight of all; it is peculiarly so to its pensioners and dependants. Of all creatures, whether in heaven or earth, man has most reason to say, How great is His goodness. We have proved its resources in a way in which perhaps they were never before proved. Creation was an act of goodness, for the design of our Maker was to multiply separate instances of happiness; it was a dissemination of His own joy. But when man, in whom was placed an extraordinary spring of happy life, affecting the well-being of the whole animal world, corrupted himself by transgression, and drew, as it were, all nature after him into misery and death, God provided a remedy to heal the world, instead of a new creation to replace it. We shall see that it was a greater act of goodness to raise the fallen world, than to push it aside for a substitute. And not goodness only, but all the attributes of God seemed to divulge new glories when they took their places in the work of redemption. They were called to evolve new features; features more sublime than had ever appeared. God disclosed *parts of His ways* that had probably never been heard of among the angels themselves. They had seen Him create a man, but they had never seen Him save a sinner. If there was ever astonishment in heaven, it must have been then, when the method of salvation began to be revealed. Holiness was never clothed in a beauty so luminous and august as when it guarded the reputation of the law which men had transgressed. Justice never shone forth with greater brightness and honor than when it demanded such an expiation for sin as was worthy the Author of that law. Love had never appeared to possess so entire a supremacy in the divine counsels as when, in the form of *mercy*, she pleaded for the arrest of the sinner's doom : and when at her pleadings, the sword was stayed, and a way of reconciliation opened between heaven and earth, it was then that the angels learned by a new and wonderful illustration that God Himself was love. Wisdom never revealed so amiable and so profound a skill as when she projected a scheme of deliverance in which all the perfections of Deity found a place and an office; where the claims of each were honored, and all could enter with rejoicing fellowship upon the enterprise of mercy. And when these counsels were known, when the details of redemption began to be unfolded, and the dimensions of the plan expanded into outline and harmony, heaven's universal host sent up a shout of praise, "loud as from numbers without number," *How great is His goodness, and how great is His beauty!*

Even an intellectual view of the Christian system must extort such an acknowledgment. It is the perfection of goodness and of beauty. But we, my brethren, have more than a pictorial representation of it. The substance, the reality of it, is ours; and its most important measures have been transacted in our world. We have seen Divine love in strange and singularly affecting circumstances. There is something saddening and, at first sight, unlovely in the humiliations to which grace descended to accomplish its work; and there are not a few who, though they consider the gospel a system of great beauty, propose to increase its attraction by removing some peculiarities, which they think distasteful or erroneous. The offensive passages they refer to are the sufferings and death of Christ, regarded as the medium of a sinner's acceptance with God! * They object to something violent and unnatural in the sacrificial features of the gospel. But when we taste the grace that flows to us through the dying of the Lord Jesus, His blood, so far from appearing an unnatural or distasteful object, becomes the most precious image of the mind. It is a source of exquisite and unfailing joy. It is the price of our salvation, and an everlasting memorial of what God could do, and what God did for us. Looking upon that, we feel the kindlings of holier dispositions; we abhor the sin that made its shedding needful; we love the heart that did not refuse to give it for us; we confide in its efficacy as the ground of our reconciliation with God, and are justified in His sight. Through it we ask for blessings, and through it we receive them. It lends to prayer a beseeching power that overcomes God Himself. It gives to our imperfect thanksgivings so fragrant an incense, that their odours fill the courts of heaven. It imparts so infinite a merit to our services, that, feeble and unworthy as they are, God accepts and honours them. Precious blood! it does all this for us,

* See Note at the end of the Volume.

and much more. We are never so impressed with the goodness of God as when we see His Divine Son dying for sinners, nor struck with the beauty of God as when we see sinners believing on His Son.

Look, first, at the work that is wrought upon the sinner's soul. It is a new creation. The heart is "without form and void," and "darkness is upon the face of its deep." You will say there is neither goodness nor beauty there. But the Spirit of God moveth upon the face of the waters. God says, "Let there be light;" and there is light; and light is the beginning of beauty. The shining of a spiritual heaven over the sinner's heart is a more glorious object than the light of the physical firmament, for it is the radiancy of Deity Himself; it is the brightness of intelligence; not created "for signs, and for seasons, and for days, and years," but ordained to hang its unfading splendours over the ages of eternity. A spirit that has recovered the likeness of God, and is arrayed in that fine linen, clean and white, of which John speaks,* will be one of the most beautiful creations of heaven. But observe, secondly, the way in which the new creature is made. The beauty of a work depends in part on its simplicity. In the

* Rev. xix. 8.

first chapter of Genesis you will perceive that the inexpressible sublimity of the creation arises from the facility with which stupendous existences follow the fiat of God. Land and sea, with their thousand varieties of life, come into being with a word; another word appoints their functions and fixes their habitations. There was no elaborate process of manufacture; it was, "Let there be light: and there was light," "Let there be a firmanent of heaven; and it was so." What a sublime representation of power, and what a beauty does it reflect upon God's works that, glorious and perfect as they are, they were begotten by a simple expression of His will! It may be remarked of nature's laws, that these are, as far as man has discovered them, exceedingly simple, the mightiest revolutions following the most insignificant means. Applying to the work of grace the principle that *simplicity* is an essential quality of beauty, where shall we find a law, at once so simple and so mighty as *faith*. A man with the accumulated sin of many years, with his habits rooted and grounded in iniquity, his passions grown irresistible by frequent indulgence, an enemy to God and to morality, one who has been gradually conformed to the image of Satan, is arrested by the Spirit, and directed to look to Jesus. He believes on the Son of God, and suddenly becomes a new creature. Go into the street which is called Straight, and inquire in the house of Judas for one who *prayeth*. Yesterday he was a fierce persecutor, lofty, proud, remorseless, bloody—but now how changed! meek, contrite, confiding; adorning the name he had despised, and loving the people he had imprisoned! And the subsequent life of Paul proves that his conversion, which was effected in a few hours, was one of *principle*, bringing with it a corresponding change of purpose, affection, and habit; moulding a character of unrivalled strength and beauty, and projecting a career of unexampled zeal, fidelity, and usefulness.

You may object to the instance of Paul, since his conversion was miraculous; but the biography of the church will furnish you with examples nearly as illustrious as that of the great apostle, in which it will be seen that faith, or the simple belief of the mind in Jesus Christ, has produced an instant and permanent change in the character, a change not only involving reconciliation with God, but a real transformation of life, without either pilgrimages or penances, fastings or mortifications. It has seemed more natural to man that virtue should be the fruit of long *endeavour*; that a revolution in our habits and tastes should be a work of time. But the law of the Gospel is, "*Believe and do;*" and on this principle it has worked all its marvels. What a mistaken philanthropy has for many generations been endeavouring to effect, Christianity has often accomplished in a few months. The gospel by its reconciling music has drawn together rude and barbarous tribes, and charmed them into order, peace, and prosperity. Villages have arisen with their churches and schools, spreading a landscape for the eye of the traveller that compels him to exclaim in praise of its Author, "How great is his goodness, and how great is his beauty!"

And O when this marvellous gospel shall have finished its design! A new heart is a beautiful object; the laws which sanction its pardon and procure its holiness are exquisitely simple; and wonderful is the process by which new features of character are introduced, and the inner man grows up God-ward, until the measuring angel can report the full stature of a man in Christ. But when God's good and beautiful Spirit raises the entire race of man to its proper height; when the members of this once honourable family, now shrunken and dispersed, are brought together by the affinities of grace, and the lowest and worst specimen of man walks erect upon the soil, a son of God; when the earth shall become one holy mountain, to the top of which every tribe shall be seen ascending to behold the beauty of the Lord and to inquire in His temple, all pressing up the grand steep of truth,—the idolater to stretch out his hands to God, the Mohammedan to transfer his homage and enthusiasm to the once hated Jesus, the Buddhist to wake up from his dream of annihilation to a certain and glorious immortality, the oppressed and brutalized African to taste the liberty of a man whom the Son makes free, and the long lost Jew, escaping from the ministration of condemnation, written and engraven in stones, to the ministration of life,—all distinctions broken down, all antipathies dissolved, the serpent creeping back into his own hell never to return, and the curse with him; the evening and the morning of the last day's labour, the last day's battle and suffering, finished, and God's eternal Sabbath shining over a new creation; then, and not until then, shall we understand *how great is His goodness, and how great is His beauty!*

SERMON XI.

Mal. iv. 2.*

" Unto you that fear my name shall the Sun of righteousness arise with healing in his wings."

In these words are represented the seasons of night and morning, and the condition of those who watch for the rising of the day, who "walk in darkness," but "fear the Lord," and have their faces turned toward the East. All upon whom the Sun of righteousness has not shined may be called the children of the *night:* but so few have welcomed the dawn of truth and heavenly love that the world may be said to lie in the blackness of spiritual night; nation by the side of nation. Upon continents, upon islands, under every sky, in every clime, the human race *sleeps.* Millions never wake! They sleep the sleep of death and pass away. Generations slumber out their age, and are then swallowed up by the "outer darkness."

But breaking the silence of this fatal repose is the stir and murmur of returning consciousness. You may hear it on every side if you

* Preached on behalf of Missions.

listen for it: men standing up stretching their faculties, benumbed by long inaction, and shaking from their spirit the languor that cleaves to a recent awakening. They are still in darkness, for the glory of the Lord has not yet risen upon them; but they are awake. No longer dreamers, they are conscious of the realities about them. Let your eye range over the populations of this vast India! A few years ago, they lay still as death, and in the gloom of death's shadow. From Cape Comorin to the Himalaya, hardly a throb of moral life could be heard. The Bramin in his refined and haughty pantheism, the Pariah in his grosser paganism, the Mohammedan in his profound fanaticism, and their two hundred million followers, in tribes, castes, orders, and schools, lay stretched upon the plains and in the valleys of Hindustan as one sleeper! insensible to the truth without, conversing only with the false dream-land within. But look at these races now. There is nearly the same darkness, but not the same torpor. The trance of idolatry is over; broken by political convulsions and by the moral force of education. Many have awakened to bewilderment, and wish themselves asleep again. They have increased sorrow in proportion as they have acquired knowledge. They cry to each other in the eagerness of their speculations, "What of the night! What of the night!" They seek to find a way by the brief lights of their own kindling; but the meteors of human theories which are struck out from the darkness, and which throw a momentary flash upon the traveller's path, only serve to make that path more erring. Still anything is better than *sleep;* and although they may wake up to misery, it is the misery of a man with his senses about him; who brings all his faculties and means into use to obtain relief, and is a ready listener to any hope of deliverance. O let us go and tell these night-wanderers that the morning cometh! You need not go far to seek them; they are to be found among educated Natives and uneducated Europeans. Theirs is a melancholy darkness, for they wait for no *day.* They know enough of God and of themselves to make them unhappy. They are dissatisfied with their own nature. They have tried, it may be, to smile away the Bible doctrines of sin and natural depravity; yet that sin has been attested by a conscience they have never been able to silence, and that depravity has hitherto defeated every effort to subdue it: the significant fact that they are averse to that which would elevate them, and love that which would debase them, perplexes and disheartens their spirit; and death with its hereafter looks upon them with no friendly face. They try to reason it all away, but it has its seasons of visitation, and neither sophistry nor vice can master it. This is *night:* its gloom, its half-consciousness, its spectres, its fears, its wearisome watchings. Is the promise of the text for these? I am happy to believe it is; for although they cannot be said to fear the Lord, not having any fixed idea of Him, they are the victims of a spiritual terror, or the subjects of an anxious inquiry after Him whom they know not: and as such, the Holy Spirit cannot be indifferent to them. If their awakening be only a *partial* consciousness of God, if their agitation be rather intellectual or social than the direct effect of gospel truth, the movement must be traced to the finger that points and rules every effect. The missionary in India rejoices to preach to the Hindu mind when aroused, and tossed to and fro by doubts and apprehensions; it is the idolater *asleep* that disheartens the preacher: invitation and warning, judgment and mercy, alike fail to disturb the marble repose of a Hindu asleep in his errors and iniquity. If the natives be stirred by *any power*, the gospel is thereby advanced, and we rejoice, yea, and will rejoice.

But let me address myself especially to those who have been awakened by the voice of the Spirit through the herald of the gospel; whose fear of the Lord is an enlightened dread of divine wrath, distinctly announced to be coming upon those who obey not the gospel; who feel the presence of a judging God, and tremble; who, under the curse of the law, consent to that law that it is *good*, and that its condemnation of them is just. These are in darkness; they have acquired divine knowledge and personal virtue—stars, shedding a cold and ineffective light that can never satisfy those who watch for the dawn. There is no warmth, no healing, in the wings of a star. There is no joy in the mere possession of a virtue; a galaxy of them can never make the sky of a man's hopes cheerful; they may decorate his character, and fascinate the observer, but they cannot gladden himself; they touch him faintly and distantly, and there are places in his soul they never reach. It is the Sun only that can fill the sphere of a man's life, penetrate the soil of his heart, and quicken into activity and cultivation the retired and interior ground of his nature. Every man is in darkness until he is "light in the Lord."

There may be in this congregation those

who are watching for the greater light that rules the day; whom God has awakened by His truth, but not yet comforted by His presence. *This then is the message which we have heard of Him, and declare unto you,* that unto such as *you,* the Sun of Righteousness will arise with healing in His wings. Blessed promise! It is the morning star seen just above the horizon, the harbinger of day. Look upon it, ye that fear the Lord and await His coming; it glitters on the eastern side of the sky. As you gaze fixedly upon it, are you not conscious of some hope and comfort, as if that part of the heaven were already lighting up with the gray approaches of morning? The prince of darkness would spread his sable wings to depress the dawn, to make the day late and tardy; but it shall come—it cannot tarry. The Bridegroom of heaven is leaving His chamber; and ere long there will be "nothing hid from the heat thereof." Grief endureth for a night, but joy cometh in the morning. Let me remind you that the restlessness and dejection you feel at the absence of the Lord is the Spirit's own work upon your conscience. But for His gracious impulse you would have been asleep still. What a mercy to have *consciousness,* even if you have no *peace!* What a mercy, that instead of running about in the wilderness of idolatrous creeds, or losing yourself in the labyrinths of a vain philosophy, you are brought, by gracious leadings, to the *sure word of prophecy*, whereunto you "take heed, as unto a light that shineth in a dark place, until the day dawn, and the day star arise in your hearts!" The promise of that star is from the Father of lights, who has put the times and the seasons in His own power, and whose word has no variableness nor shadow of turning. My dear friends in darkness, let me lead you to the place where the Sun rises; and there let us stand together, until His earliest ray glance upon our spirits, and the glory of the Lord be risen upon us. Let us all go, unitedly and confidently; let the children of the day accompany us, to obtain a clearer and fuller view of Christ as He rises once more over Calvary; for it is the gazer's privilege to approach nearer and nearer this Star of the East, to look more stedfastly and narrowly upon the transforming light, until he is "changed into the same image from glory to glory, even as by the Spirit of the Lord."

But there are some who doubt whether they have any ground to expect that the morning will rise upon *them*. I hear them say that no darkness which I have described is to be matched with the gloom that has settled down upon their spirits; that having once rejoiced in the happy light of God's favour, theirs is the sevenfold darkness of *contrast*, and a contrast chargeable upon their own folly and sin. Oh there is no shadow so appalling as the backslider's night! it is not merely the absence of the sun, but a horrible eclipse; for the soul that is dark, had once its place in the sphere and firmament of the church. John informs us that he saw a great star fall from heaven, whose name was Wormwood; and that the waters into which it fell became wormwood, and those who drank thereof died. So, when a Christian falls from the heaven of God's countenance, he becomes wormwood, and like a blasting planet he infects, poisons, and destroys the souls of other men. St. Jude uses a similar figure when speaking of backsliders, *Wandering Stars;* that is, stars that have withdrawn from the central Sun of Righteousness; to whom, says he, is reserved the blackness of darkness for ever. Is there among my hearers a soul whose name is Wormwood, who is yet falling from God into deeper night? And is such a spirit looking up with the anguish of a longing heart to the place he once filled with the morning stars and the sons of God? The attraction of that

Sun can arrest a falling orb, and bring back the dark wanderer into the shining paths of the just; and therefore I must encourage even the backslider to wait with us, and hope for the marvellous light of pardon and love that shines upon all who watch for it.

Let us now consider the promise more particularly, The Sun of Righteousness shall arise with healing in His wings.

Sun of Righteousness, is not so much a figurative designation of the Lord Jesus Christ, as a name strictly implying His nature and offices. When He stood on this earth, He announced Himself as *the light of the world;* and as His orb ascended from the obscurity of Judea, and gained the altitude of His mission, as His line went forth into all the earth, and His words unto the end of the world, dividing the light from the darkness, He absorbed within Himself all the lesser lights and gleams of science and virtue, and blazed forth the undisputed sovereign of the moral heaven. He glanced upon the schools of paganism, and learned Gentiles came to His light; He penetrated and awed the majesty of thrones, and kings hailed the brightness of His rising. Yet the light which He dispensed was not the lustre of intellect, but of righteousness, of holiness. His doctrines flattered not the vanity of the learned, but assailed that vanity. He did not, like the philosophers, preach the greatness of the human mind, and exalt it as a divinity to be worshipped; but His teaching conducted the eye into man's heart, exposing its deceitfulness, its uncleanness, its baseness. It dissected the opinions and institutions of men; laid bare the folly of their hopes, the treachery of their supports, the unsatisfying nature of their resources. It unsettled many of their maxims, reversed some of their most confident conclusions, showed the extent of their ignorance of heavenly things, and opened through the mazes of sin, hitherto impenetrable, a pathway to God.

Herein does Christ vindicate for Himself the glorious title of *Sun of Righteousness*. He discovered and brought to light the highway to heaven. He provided a righteousness which could give the dying sinner a title to life. Whereas men's terrors drove them to every method of atonement that convicted guilt could devise, Jesus became a propitiation for them all. Men might now cast off their superstitious yokes, throw down their altars, and escape the hard despotism of a slavish fear. He preached liberty without the captive's effort, redemption without a price, and eternal happiness without desert. " By *grace* are we saved, through faith, and that not of ourselves, it is the gift of God." It was Christ only who could say, and the words were *the key-note of His ministry*,* "Blessed are they that hunger and thirst after righteousness, for they shall be filled." This was the world's condition when Christ first appeared, it hungered and thirsted for righteousness. No system had as yet been revealed by which man could obtain it. There was everything but *righteousness;* but this is the same as if we should say of the physical world, there is everything but *light*. Let the sun cease to shine upon us, even for a few months, let moon and stars withdraw their light, let this earth revolve through blackness and darkness; if it were possible for life itself to survive, would life be worth having? Would it not be all the horrors and hell of *death*, without its happy insensibility? The desire of the senses would be gone; the soul would be a dungeon without windows; human progress would not merely stop, but society would freeze up into an iceberg. Its fellowships, its enterprises, its grand organs of intercourse, its skill, benevolence, and potency, would drift away like the snow of an avalanche, cold, scattered and meaningless. We should still have our gold and silver,

* Trench.

our precious stones, our books, pictures, and instruments of music; but these are a mockery without light. Property has no valuation, music no motive, for who would touch a harp? books are blotted out, and pictures, the children of light, are dead—

> Nor public flame, nor private, dares to shine;
> Nor human spark is left, nor glimpse divine!
> Lo! thy dread empire, Chaos! is restored;
> Light dies before thy uncreating word;
> Thy hand, great Anarch! lets the curtain fall;
> And universal darkness buries all.

A moral world without Christ, is like a physical world without the sun. That which can draw a human being up to the primary stature of a man, is the transforming light of holy truth; this is the educating light; it shines down in direct rays from heaven; it is warm, healing, and genial; man's soul is like a kindred beam, darting forth to meet it; it will blend with no other light. The mind that shines not in the beauty of holiness can never be made beautiful by other accomplishments. The proper definition of a *man* is, an intelligent being created after God in righteousness and true holiness; and our unhappy race can never be lifted from its degeneracy, will never display those sublime capacities of thinking, governing, and enjoying, of which we see but faint indications now, will never explain the meaning of man's creation at all, until minor illuminations be swallowed up in the glory of righteousness; until this original light resume its sway, and become the prevailing medium of man's perceptions, the guide and gladness of man's path. One of the most generally discussed questions of the day relates to *the improvement of the masses.* I honor the philanthropy that addresses itself to the poor; abridging their hours of toil, increasing their wages, educating their children, cleansing their neighbourhoods, and promoting their access to institutions of learning and recreation; but unless we make the gospel of Christ the foundation of our efforts, we build man's improvement on the sand; at any moment a revolutionary storm might bring the structure upon our heads. When your missionaries have gone forth to countries where men have been found verging upon the rudeness of the beast, they have not raised them by secular arts *first*, and grafted righteousness upon civilization; they have begun their work by bringing them to Christ; and when these rude half-formed spirits drank in the rays of the *Sun of Righteousness*, they put forth the graces of social life; their unripe and childish ideas expanded into the enterprises of men; communities were gathered and knit into shape and order; the school was established; the plough introduced; law and protection followed; and the peaceful hum of village life now greets the stranger where once his footsteps would have been tracked by the scent of blood. Righteousness is at once the foundation and the crown of a nation. Where Christ shines not, nothing that is truly noble attains maturity. Science, education, and genius, are rather great powers that flourish in the light, than light itself. Of that perfect society which is described as heaven, the celestial city into which will be gathered all that is precious in intellect, friendship, and character; all that is venerable for wisdom, admirable for strength, lovely for beauty, it is said, *the glory of God enlightens it, and the Lamb is the light thereof.*

This is the Sun of Righteousness, and the promise is unto you that He will arise with healing in His rays. Let us now look toward that quarter of the heavens, where we expect Him to appear. He rises over the Cross; that is our East. Draw near, ye timid souls, and await His coming; tread out the sparks of your own righteousness; distrust in this path the light of reason—an unsafe guide here. Whatever visions may dance before your eye, believe that you are in utter darkness until Christ shines; believe not the suggestions of your own heart—believe its necessities and its misery; it may tell you you are too dark to be enlightened; you have had too long a night ever to hope for morning; your misery is too complicated and inveterate even for the healing light of the Gospel to remedy: answer all such misgivings by the promise of the text, Unto you that fear My name; unto you that, after many failures, are convinced at last that you cannot walk by the light of your own understanding, or stand in the strength of your own resolutions; unto you that, after trying every method to obtain satisfaction and peace, now find yourselves without a sin conquered, a fear dispelled, a wish realized, a hope accomplished; mortified, humbled, crushed, shut up to what GOD can do for you,—unto you *shall the Sun of Righteousness arise with healing in His wings.* Doubt not the word, even though you may not fully comprehend it; believe it, it will bring its own meaning with it. Jesus will rise upon your souls like a glorious dawn. You want no preparation but a waiting heart. The flower gives nothing to the sun for shining upon it; and the Lord God will give you grace and glory, without money and without price.

SERMON XII.

2 Tim. ii. 3.*

"Endure hardness as a good soldier of Jesus Christ."

This exhortation was addressed to a young missionary, who, like you, had been recently set apart by the laying on of hands for the good fight of ministerial life. It is the counsel of a veteran, whose career, from the hour of his enlistment, had been a grand conflict with the powers of darkness, and whose battle was closing with victory. He had striven for masteries, had won them, and was now returning to his sovereign to receive those distinctions which are promised to loyalty, courage, devotion, and hard service. But though he had secured *his* crown, the fight was not over. The field was as crowded as ever with hostility and danger; and others must fill up ranks which death or infirmity had thinned. We can imagine that Paul would be anxious to secure for a small but eminently aggressive church, able, energetic,

* Preached at the ordination of a missionary.

and holy men. Upon Timothy he had laid no sudden hands. The selection of missionaries should be a task of solemn deliberation. The first apostles attempted no proceeding of this kind without an especial appeal to the Holy Ghost. They fasted, prayed, and waited to receive a direct intimation of the Divine will. They then laid their hands upon the man after God's own heart, and sent him about his work. The two epistles to Timothy compose an impressive charge, to the study of which every minister should devote his life. I have no doubt you have often read and paused over these inimitable compositions, so full of sagacious counsels, wise cautions, and invigorating hopes; and if by this address I can recall some of them to your memory, and add any remark which may increase the influence they have upon your character, I shall have the result for which I have laboured and prayed.

You will perceive that the apostle delivers his lesson in military language. Timothy is called *a soldier of Jesus Christ*. We have no other mode of describing the operation of principles opposed to each other, than borrowing the language of external warfare; and when not principles merely, but *spirits* are drawn up in battle array, thinking against each other, planning schemes for each other's ruin, and wielding the dreadful weapons of the mind, military phrases are scarcely adequate to the description of such a conflict. The scriptures abound in martial allusions. Christ is *the leader and commander of His people*, who are commonly described as an armed host, contending for every inch of ground that lies between them and their own land, to which they are represented as returning through a country bristling with enemies, prepared to dispute their passage; and not simply travelling through the hostile land with the negative resistance of an orderly retreat, but falling upon their foes aggressively, to win territory and captives for their sovereign. Every Christian is a man of war from the commencement of his journey to heaven, and there is no retirement from service, no quiet evening of his days in which he may enjoy a laurelled repose; he lays down his weapons and his life together. This condition of strife and contest applies with special force to the preachers of the Cross—above all to *missionaries;* for these may be said to conquer a province, and ordinary ministers to garrison it. If the harder service is the more honorable, what distinction has the great Captain conferred upon you, in assigning to you a front position in the army that is marching *to the help of the Lord against the mighty!* I hope you have well considered the trust which has been confided to you; I hope you have not now to be told that the spot upon which you stand is thickest with danger; and that a man behaving treasonably or cowardly here, hurts the cause for which we fight, more than the fall of a thousand elsewhere. Glory and infamy are side by side; therefore "endure hardness as a good soldier of Jesus Christ."

Endure the hardness of the march. The march is often more trying to bravery than the engagement. Your march is the intellectual and moral *preparation* that leads you to the field and arms you for battle. Endure the hardness of *study*. Your enemy lies on the other side of a foreign and difficult language; and through an almost impenetrable jungle of superstitions. Master these! In respect of the preliminaries of the language, you are more fortunate than we are, the ground being more familiar to you, and the obstacles fewer; but as you approach the heart of its literature our labors are equal;. and it will cost you the exertion and patience it imposes upon us. I do not think *eminent* scholarship essential to the evangelist; but language is your path to a man's heart; and the more extensive and minute your acquaintance with the tongue he speaks, the more readily will you convey the arguments and facts which God has enjoined you to communicate to him. In preaching to the Hindus, it is not enough that you be able to speak the native tongue with fluency. By a diligent reading of purely vernacular books, you must acquire those idiomatic or characteristic forms of speech that give such a charm to conversation and discourse. I need not tell you of the itching ears with which Hindu people listen to the man who proposes to instruct them; and while we ought not to shape our sentences to tickle and gratify a passion for ornament, it becomes us to avoid disgusting it by barbarisms, or fatiguing it by triteness and inanity. In studying the religion of the Hindus, while you have no ambition to excel in the curious learning of Indian sages,—nor is it necessary in order to become an able vernacular minister,—you will do well to lay hold of the vulnerable points of the native's faith, the more obvious and refutable errors of his system. For these will be found generally to lie near its foundation; and in this study, place the errors you find side by side with scripture and with your own nature; read the book of God and the book of your own heart together, and you will discover that idolatry is alike unscriptural and unnatural. Adopt no views which you yourself have not proved; use no phrases which you have not married to your own thought; hazard no statements that you yourself cannot show to be facts. Study thoroughly those parts of Hinduism which are the strongholds of its defence; study them in the bazaars as well as in the Shasters; let your observation gather something every day that may serve to point an argument or enforce a lesson. The best account of Hinduism, however, will be found not in the Puranas, but in the Bible. Here you have, in the words of the Holy Ghost Himself, its origin and growth; and such revelations of the fallen heart of man as every conscience verifies. If you aim to be a faithful and swift witness against the wickedness and errors of this people, *endure the hardness of Bible study*. The Bible reading of a missionary is hard and solemn work. If it be anything else in the case of such a man, it is a levity. God has spoken words for the heathen; He has, I trust, made you a chosen vessel to bear them to the Gentiles of India. How can you enforce words you understand not? And how can you succeed in grasping, and making available, meanings that come up from eternity and the Divine mind, unless you think with almost prophetic intensity, and pray with the commanding faith of a Daniel, to whose supplications God unlocked the secrets of His providence and name? Oh! to take up one of God's messages, which you feel you must deliver; to pause over it with assiduous and watchful meditation—to bring upon it the various lights of a sanctified erudition; to be still dark as to its import, and in darkness to go to the Father of lights, and to plead for the return of the inspiration by which it was first given; to kneel beside it with a stedfast eye, and wait, until the thing of darkness is brought to light, and the counsel of the Most High is manifest; and then, as a steward of the mystery, to take it, and make it intelligible to the ignorant and brutish mind of a heathen—to make it pass through processes of thought and illustration until not merely the pupil that sits at your feet and hears it again and again, but the wayfaring man who may not have the opportunity of hearing it the second time, shall be able to understand it!—this is the hardness of the missionary's Bible study, and involves an application at once active, patient, laborious, and sanguine; to which only those will submit who are *constrained by the love of Christ.* There are other motives that may prompt a man to great exertion in his studies: a desire for distinction or emolument, a taste for the discoveries of knowledge or the elegancies of art, will make a scholar; but no motive except the love of Jesus can make a *missionary*. There are so many discouragements in his path, and his progress through it is so slow, and it seems such a long and mountainous way to success,

    Alps peep o'er Alps, and hills on hills arise,—

his own earthly mind, a constant fear of unfaithfulness, shocks of bodily illness diminishing his strength, domestic troubles, and, above all, the apathy, perverseness, and wickedness of the heathen, that no ordinary fortitude could withstand such hardships; and these trials will be yours. In endeavoring to cope with them, many have fallen; and he only overcomes whose *sufficiency is of God*. When we are in the actual fight, when we close with an adversary in the presence and amid the cheers of others, zeal and enthusiasm sustain us; it is in the sterner road of private life that we generally fail. Be watchful in the quiet march. Let not your missionary life be a life of occasions. I mean a life that exists not except there be a public and inevitable service to call it forth. A soldier discharges all his duties in drill, whether there be an enemy or not. It is the private discipline of the camp that nurses the heroism of the field. Therefore, my dear brother, bring your spirit into severe training. Keep always before you the dispositions and habits in which you feel yourself lacking. When no eye but God's sees you, strive to cultivate them; it will often cost you a struggle to maintain a heavenly mind—to cherish and practice industry in study, economy in domestic life, conscientiousness in business, and painstaking preparation for public work. Let your retired interviews with God be so frequent, as to form the grand necessity of your life. As far as the earthly tabernacle will permit you, live in heaven; and, if possible, do not stand up in the people's midst, until the angel that waits upon the altar of inspiration has taken a coal and laid it upon your mouth, and you have heard him say, " Lo, this hath touched thy lips; thine iniquity is taken away and thy sin purged!"

Endure the hardness of the actual fight. The missionary's fight is a hard battle. He begins by conquering himself on the march, and in proportion to the power by which he has subdued the province of his own heart, will be the strength of his arm against the foe, and the chance of his victory. The enemy led up against you is the colossal system of Hinduism, animated by the cunning and pride of Satan. The poor idolater himself is not an adversary. You must beware lest in discussion or preaching, any unfriendly sentiment should escape you; lest the contempt which you must feel for the *absurdities*, should show itself towards the *victims* of superstition. You have no quarrel with the Hindu; and you must guard against the faintest semblance of personal enmity. In a missionary's arguments, love is more potent than logic; and though it is sometimes expedient to ridicule a sophism, in order to shame a disputant whom vanity has made your opponent, irony and satire rarely become the messenger of Christ. Men's errors are not purely intellectual; in the case of a Hindu they have no more to do with the understanding than as that faculty may be exercised in the habits that perpetuate them. No religionist, save the Christian, can give a reason for the hope that is within him. The prevailing temper of the preacher who denounces idolatry, should be pity; not the spurious compassion that looks down upon its object from a platform of superiority, but the pity of Jesus; the tenderness of the elder brother for a younger; the pity that men call weakness, the charity that beareth all things. It burned in Christ's heart when he shed tears over Jerusalem; in Paul's heart when he wept over backsliders. Pray earnestly and constantly that the spirit of love may pervade your addresses to the heathen. It will expand your exhortations, it will lay your intellect, your acquisitions, and all your appliances under tribute; and draw them into one strain of irresistible persuasion to induce men to be *reconciled to God*. It is hard to love those who hate God and you; it is hard to pursue a sinner, especially the phlegmatic and deceitful Hindu, through his contemptible defences of himself and of what he believes; to endure the indifference of a conscience which every truth fails to disturb; to contend with your own doubts as to whether God himself can bring such a mind to the knowledge of the truth; and when you have succeeded so far as to produce an apparent impression, and have followed it up by careful and anxious teaching, how painful, how sickening to find in the end, that what you mistook for a *conviction of the truth*, was a *trick* practised upon your credulity! Endure the hardness of returning from false ground, and fighting your battles over again. You leave the enemy dead upon the field, as you imagine; but while you are chanting your victory song, he revives, and renews the attack! There is perhaps no duty in the missionary's career that makes so urgent a demand upon his valour, as the endurance of exertions consequent upon failure and disappointment. It resembles *bush fighting*, where the soldier must ever be on the alert; for at any moment he may be laid low by an unseen hand, and can seldom strike a blow himself. Prepare for this species of reverse; remember that the battle is not yours, but the Lord's. Your efforts may appear to yourself to go but a little way, but you are not answerable for results, you are answerable only for courage, zeal, and fidelity. See that *you* fail not; leave all consequences with God. Be you ever so successful, *it is not by might, nor by power, but by the Spirit of the Lord*, that the engagement is to prosper, and the field to be won. The fight is a fight of *faith*: take your confidence, not from appearances, but from promises which are *yea and amen*. Strive to realize the presence of Him who goes before you with the two-edged sword and the undrooping arm; glue one hand to the banner of the cross and the other to the weapon of the Spirit: quit you like a man, be strong; so shall the enemy flee before you, and his strongholds tremble!

But other trials await you in the actual fight. You begin your career in a critical time. It seems to me that conflicts of no ordinary severity await the Indian missionary. There has been for a long time a silent undermining of the native religions of this country; and the work has advanced with uncommon rapidity during the last two years. The people are becoming thoroughly awakened to the dangers that threaten their faith, their customs, their venerated institutions. Recent disturbances are symptoms of a profound antagonism, and must awaken anxiety in the mind of every missionary. An open declaration of the gospel in the presence of the heathen is no longer the quiet task our fathers found it; it cannot now be boldly made, without risk; and this risk may grow more perilous. If you would fulfil your ministry *faithfully*, you must not only part with your convenience, but often expose the security of your person or dwelling; nay, be subject to a more terrible class of perils, the scorn of pride, and the misrepresentations of malice. Woe be unto you if you shun danger, when danger lies between you and perishing souls. *He that loveth his life shall lose it; he that loses his life for Christ's sake shall find it unto life eternal.* If you are conscious of timidity in the presence of Hindus, and are tempted to soften the strictness of your message in order to make your errand easy and safe, to cry *peace* when God has not spoken peace, deplore before the Almighty Judge a weakness that may ruin your soul. Forget *yourself* in this high calling. What matter if you or I should be called to suffer for Jesus: we have no personal importance whatever: our life is only worth preserving as long as it can render any service to Christ. The subject that fills our thoughts, and awakens our care and solicitude should be Christ and not self. *Self* we have long ago dedicated to Him, and He is able to keep it, and will Himself answer for its well being. That which you must look well to is the trust committed to you; to bear the gospel of Redeeming love to the heathen. It matters not when or in what manner you are called to lay it down; it may be early in your career, or late; it may be violently in an outburst of persecution; it may be peaceably in your own house; it may be suddenly in the midst of hopeful labour; it may be lingeringly in the furnace of slow disease. What matters it? God will never lay you aside, until He can do without you. Go with this confidence, and execute your trust. What can man do unto *you?* Yours is a charmed life until you have finished your work. Think frequently with yourself when you are preaching to the heathen, "This word is not *mine*, but Jehovah's who has sent me; my soul contains it and my mouth gives it forth; I am simply accountable for the fidelity with which I deliver it." This reflection, habitually cherished, will give authority to your word, and a holy fortitude to your spirit. God can bring strength out of weakness; the feeblest and most timid soldier of His army may become by faith a hero, and laugh at impossibilities!

Let me say in conclusion, prepare yourself for no ordinary career. You will be a great success or a great failure. You may pass a quiet, respectable, and well-reputed life, among men, and God may be ashamed of you; or you may live without notice,—obscure, afflicted, and despised, and be the glory of Christ. While the Master gives you work to do, do it thoroughly, unflinchingly, and with high conscientiousness. *Preach the word; be instant in season, out of season. Watch in all things, endure afflictions; do the work of an evangelist, make full proof of thy ministry. And when the chief Shepherd shall appear, thou shalt receive a crown of glory that fadeth not away.*

SERMON XIII.

1 PETER iii. 8.

"*Be courteous.*"

THERE is no feature of the Christian system that so impressively attests its divine birth as the universality of its provisions. The more liberally we study it, the more clearly it discovers the comprehensiveness as well as the truth of Nature herself. Other forms of sacred belief contemplate but a partial development of the human character; and as the religious feelings are the most imperious of our sentiments, it follows that, when thus excited by a narrow faith, they distort the mind; bringing out some of its powers, and depressing others. In Hinduism he is esteemed the perfect man who can *endure* the most for religion; in Mohammedanism, he who can *do* the most. Both heroes disdain ordinary virtues. The devotee of Siva scourges and starves himself in the wilderness; the Mussulman, if the Prophet gives him an opportunity, rushes into the field and takes the life of the infidel or loses his own: but each will violate truth and honesty; and contemn that genuine love of our kind which is the parent of friendship, fidelity, courtesy, and their kindred amenities.

Christianity has been charged with the same one-sidedness, the same encouragement of the heroic virtues, to the prejudice of the common and more necessary morals of life. But this accusation has been preferred by those who have studied her parties instead of her doctrines. It must be granted that the annals of Christian sects exhibit shocking pictures of infirmity and crime. We blush to think of the malignity, the ambition, the hypocrisy, the bigotry, and the lust, which have so often polluted the fame and darkened the vicissitudes of the visible Christian church. But such evils are not due to the religion of Jesus; they have sprung from the Braminism and Mohammedanism of Christian professors, from the ascetic and voluptuary elements which share between them the votaries of every false faith. During the ages in which a corrupted priesthood used the church as a carnal instrument to advance their order, only such doctrines of religion were published as, by an easy perversion, excused the enormous impositions of the clergy. Under this administration the gentler, the diviner features of our blessed faith were veiled, while its sterner qualities were invested with a rigour they were never intended to assume. If mercy appeared, it was to licence indulgence; if judgment, it was to wait upon ambition; if jealousy was awakened for the defence of the truth, it was to imprison it; if zeal to maintain the discipline of the church, it was to execute plans of revenge. Those who have classed the doctrines and rites of the gospel with the abominations of paganism, have generally been indebted for their impressions to Popery. But behold Christianity as she rises from the grave of her humiliation, clothed in the pure vestment of truth, with every feature in natural symmetry, and every grace visible! Is she not *the King's daughter, all glorious within?*

There is one property which is the original distinction of the religion of Jesus. Founded on love, the doctrines of the Cross produce love to God and love to man. This is *not* the sentiment of other faiths. Their connecting principle is an attachment to a local creed and a particular people. Christianity has no prescribed home; is the peculiar heritage of no nation. It is true she prevails in some lands, and scarcely touches others; but this is the incidental partiality of *progress;* like the beginning of the sun's march, whose first footprints are seen in the east, when the yet unvisited west is in the dark. Christianity is the necessity of *mankind*, and the system is traversing the race to make that race one family. You may trace to its influence every movement whose aim is to make men and nations touch each other. Christian doctrines and predictions are abroad; they are expounded and proclaimed under different names by every school of patriotism and politics; the monarchist and the republican, the deist and the missionary, profess to dissolve antipathies and to make all men brothers. Let a man's opinions be what they may, take him from Peru or Japan, from Europe or from India, he will confess that a union of the hearts of all men would realize his idea of the millenium; for this is the simple voice of human nature. In Christian countries this voice has become a principle, an opinion; and the most strenuous efforts are being made to facilitate transit from land to land, and intercourse between people and people. The steamer, the railway, the telegraph, are so many protests against disunion: and they utter a glorious resolution, that oceans and hills, languages and faiths, castes and feuds, shall no longer divide brethren; that hostilities shall cease, that bigotry shall die, that war shall exchange his sword for the ploughshare, and his spear for the pruning-hook.

These demonstrations for union are the necessary result of the Christian doctrine that man should love man, and of the Christian prediction that man *will* love man. Our nature answers to them, every human being feels that they are true : but *we* feel also that as Christianity originated them, Christianity only can accomplish them; we feel, let it not be in a boastful spirit, that the possibility of the world's union rests with *us*. The deist, the politician, and some other philanthropists, have adopted the idea, and they exhibit it and ask support for it as *their* offspring; but they can do nothing with it upon any principles of their own : were every man a deist, or a mere patriot, it would die. It wants an agency commensurate with its aim; and such a power is furnished by the omnipotent Spirit who dwells in the hearts of Christians, and gives efficacy to Christian operations; and the *ground* upon which He works out the idea, will convince any one who considers it that no other method could possibly accomplish the union of all hearts.

He finds us divided; distributed into peoples, nations, and tongues; He goes down through the conventional separations of distance, language, color, and caste, to the basis of this division; He finds it in *selfishness*, the simple result of a divorce from God. When man could no longer trust his Maker, his mind made a stay of *itself;* clung to its own resources with the tenacious eagerness and jealousy of him who grasps a last prop. Of all that contributed to self he became covetous; of all that was alien to it, suspicious; and to retain his control of it, he closed up the originally noble sympathies of his soul, and grew reserved, deceitful, cruel. Brotherhood was gone; no two men so affected could live together, unless each imagined that himself would derive an advantage from the connection; and mutual selfishness would be the tacit bond of the union. Thus were men driven asunder, banded into tribes and peoples; and mountains rose between them, and oceans bore them to different shores, and localities gave them different names and different interests: *strangers* were enemies, and that which should have been a visit was an invasion; and war, selfish, bloody war was born, and became an inmate of men's hearts; and man armed himself with weapons, and strengthened his home with bulwarks to defend himself against his brother!

Now the ground upon which the Spirit of

Christ unites men is the primal bond of their relationship to God. He does not explain away their antipathies by teaching them that they are the children of one Father and ought to love as brethren; He does not propose that they should learn each other's language, exchange each other's produce, and visit each other's country. These are the lessons of the philanthropist, whose theories are founded upon our common birth and common rights; but the Spirit of Christianity restores a higher bond before He enforces this secondary union. He joins men where their separation from each other began; He draws them to God *first;—Thou shalt love the Lord thy God with all thy heart, and thy neighbour as thyself.* This holy and re-uniting passion is awakened at the CROSS; and when man stands before that image of himself, and learns that it is the humiliation of God, a shame into which His love for lost and scattered men prompted Him to descend; when he learns that the Creator whose authority he had renounced, whose curse he had merited, was the first to propose reconciliation, and that to negotiate and effect it He had made himself human, and was hanging there in the place of those He had condemned, so illustrious an example of love subdues his selfish heart; and by the help of the blessed

Spirit who opened his eyes upon that sight, he restores to his Maker a lost affection and a lost trust, and pledges them by a second covenant unspeakably more binding than the first.

The man who so loves God must give hand and heart to his fellow. He has no motive to refuse them; he cannot fear, therefore he has no suspicion; he will not covet, for he has ceased to live for himself; he cannot desert, for the law of love and the example of the Cross make him, insensibly, his brother's keeper, and the two become one in interest, in right, in destiny.

That this destruction of selfishness is the leading design of Christianity, and that it is the experience of all who are brought under its power, may be proved by the following passages from the New Testament;—*Ye are not your own: for ye are bought with a price. He died for all, that they which live should not henceforth live unto themselves, but unto Him which died for them and rose again. None of us liveth unto himself;—whether we live, we live unto the Lord: and whether we die, we die unto the Lord. Hereby perceive we the love of God, because he laid down His life for us: and we ought to lay down our lives for the brethren.* This surrender of ourselves for the advantage of others, which can only be practised under the operation of Christian influence, is regarded in all creeds, and by all men, as the highest human virtue. Its aspect is so charming that all men reverence and assume it. They observe its forms and speak its language; they designate it good-breeding, politeness, complaisance, courtesy. Visit an assembly. How the members of the party appear to defer to each other, as if every one preferred the honor and comfort of his neighbour to his own! The kindest, the gentlest words in the language circulate there; and although each person knows that the other *cannot mean* what he says, it affects not the apparent harmony of society: and the behaviour can hardly be called a deception, for no one can be deceived where all know and tacitly permit the cheat. In fact, the language and attitude of courtesy are the bonds of society. What a splendid testimony this to courtesy itself! If the world does homage to its likeness, if men make its *images* their household-gods, with what respect should we gaze upon, with what eagerness should we seek to possess, the *original!* Genuine courtesy is the aspect of brotherly love, and our meek and lowly Master, who knew the world perfectly, has affirmed that courtesy shall win the world to the acknowledgment of the truth. " By this shall all men know that ye are my disciples if ye love one another." The world can only judge of Christian love by its courtesy; it cannot look within our hearts; it cannot be admitted to our communion; its blunt understanding can only appreciate a palpable manifestation of love; and this is courtesy. The world knows that its own politeness is a show, that courtesy is a *mask* which every man takes down and puts on when he leaves his chamber. The meaning of our Lord's words appears to be this, if the men of the world could see a courtesy, simple, natural, sincere, the *fruit* of brotherly love, it would be convinced that God must be its author; that the wisdom which is " pure, peaceable, gentle, easy to be intreated, full of mercy and good fruits, without partiality and without hypocrisy," *must be from above*.

Christian brethren! I address those in whose hands is the argument which shall bring the world to the truth. You may be orthodox, earnest, prayerful, and active; you must be all this if you are the people of God; but the world will not care for your doctrines, and your fervour they will pronounce enthusiasm: *be pitiful, be courteous, love as brethren*, and the world will understand you, and glorify God in you. Christians have departed from this rule. We have been apt to make Christianity an object of dread to the world; we have too much concealed her gentle forgiving spirit behind a formidable array of dogmas, institutes, and orders; we have made the walls of Zion bristle with exactions and warnings, as if it were a city besieged, instead of a city of refuge; as if it were intended to keep men out, instead of inviting them in. It is not meant that there should be any compromise of law, any relaxation of discipline. For the church is an establishment and there must be order; she has enemies and must defend herself. But we insist that since her mission to the world is a mission of *love*, this feature should beam upon those that are without. If the obstinacy and wickedness of sinners compel us to announce the judgments of heaven, let this ungracious task be a mission of tears. Let us weep with the brokenhearted Redeemer when He pronounced a curse on Jerusalem.

Christians have also erred in this respect in their intercourse with each other. The reason is to be found in the low state of our personal godliness. We cannot manifest the courtesy of religion unless we have the love of Christ. I do not mean a *conviction* that we ought to possess it, but the emotion itself. Where this love exists, it resembles a nervous, darting, impatient light. If the senator has it, it is apt to throw a gleam over his speeches and measures; if it burns within the heart of the merchant, it lights up his transactions, and impresses the nature of God even upon the unspiritual enterprises of commerce; its testimony is never equivocal, its witness is never dumb.

What hurt does Christianity receive from those whose character gives an uncertain sound! Who, when they speak to them that are without, are proud, selfish, exacting, and irritable; who deal out kind words as a miser circulates his money, by single coins, and then with a tolerable certainty of receiving them back with usury; who address their servants as if they were cattle, and their equals as if they were enemies; who fill up the pauses of life with uncharitable gossip, instead of prayer and deeds of charity; who seem not to have a suspicion that they were born to suffer and to serve; to exhibit the patience, gentleness, humility, and courtesy of Jesus; to have words of love for all, for the meanest. How different *His* spirit who said, *Learn of Me, for I am meek and lowly in heart.* None knew the human heart so profoundly as He; none looked upon it so pitifully. How patiently He endured the hatred and violence of enemies; with how meek a silence He bowed to the unkindness, ingratitude, and treachery of professed friends! He never uttered an uncharitable word, was never surprised into a hasty expression : He preached, exemplified, and died for, a religion of love. When His followers are more thoroughly imbued with love, and manifest its purity, patience, and courtesy in the details of every day life, then the blessed doctrines of the Cross will be clothed with a new and practical power, that shall compel an admiration for their beauty, an acknowledgment of their necessity, and ultimately the adoption and reign of their principles.

SERMON XIV.

MATT. xv. 8.

"*Their heart is far from me.*"

OF those results of sin that afflict human society, the loss of honesty is the most affecting and disastrous. All men were first made to be brothers, having one heart in common and a transparent intercourse. The structure of our minds and the nature and capacity of our sympathies were fashioned for truthfulness of conversation and unsuspecting trust. The *lie* is not an original offspring of the mind; it is not like covetousness, intemperance, and many other sins, the abuse of primitive instincts; it is a *perversion*, at once devilish and unnatural, of the ordinary channels of expression, consequent upon a craven fear of each other engendered by the father of lies. "When he speaketh a lie," says our Saviour, with His exact knowledge, "he speaketh of *his own*."

As a proof that a lie is a sort of prodigy in vice, its tendency is to break up society, and were it thoroughly to prevail, intercourse would be at an end. Men are compelled to be true in their transactions, if there be little truth in their heart. Public confidence is the cement of communities, and public courtesy* smoothes the inequalities and irritations of society. We cannot live together without the forms of truthfulness, without drawing near unto each other with our mouth and honoring each other with our lips. Moreover, how universally the lie is disowned! A falsehood inflicts a deadlier wound upon a man's character, than almost any other crime; and " liar " is perhaps the most dreaded blot in the pollutions of infamy. A person may be intemperate and immoral, yet pass for a man of honor; but so largely do the pleasures and advantages of intercourse depend upon outward truthfulness, that he is denied the inner circles of friendship whose word is known to be insecure. There is another consideration that helps to brand the man who stoops to be false. Manliness, or the becoming dignity of a human being, is supposed to consist in the courage to hazard all for the truth; to speak it out and to maintain it. To be untrue is to be base.

But is it not a painful thought that this homage to truth is commonly little more than expediency to serve the purposes of compact

* See Sermon xiii.

between man and man. I do not mean that all who tell the truth reckon upon the profit of it: but habits of truth-doing and forms of truth-speaking have descended to us and enter into the formation of society carrying no heart with them; for how true it is, and let us look boldly at the fact, that the conversation of men, tricked out with every variety of polite expression, is *unreal;* not the voice of the soul, but the voice of the symbol. We have an excellent stock of smooth greetings, and affecting farewells; of touching condolences, and generous felicitations; but the heart is far from them. We rarely, if ever, intend mischief; but we do not mean all we say, nor feel all we mean. The expression is often the reverse of the sentiment; and so subtle is the operation of deceit, that when, for the time, we believed in our own sincerity, a little reflection afterwards convinced us that we were only acting a part.

Now every man is apt to try another by the possibilities or experiences of his own nature; and believing that his fellow does the same by him, each tries to surpass the other in the arts of deception; and this rivalry produces imitations of genuineness so exquisitely fine, that it is impossible to detect the counterfeit. Thus, *Every man walketh in a vain shew,* and, *All the world's a stage.* In commerce, in diplomacy, and in the contests of war and litigation, dissembling is an accomplishment: it is provoked by competition, and verily, *it has its reward:* but, alas! men cannot leave it behind them when they quit these stormier scenes for the retreats of life. Hypocrisy surrounds us like an atmosphere: in the drawing-room, in the friendly circle, wherever we are gathered together, for whatever purpose, there is a deplorable masking of the heart. Every one feels it; every one professes to mourn it; every one contributes to it. We meditate no deceit; but the artificial signs of kindness and truth that we find in use, we adopt: for the avowal of the heart is forbidden and almost impossible; and before we are aware of it, we discover ourselves repeating the speeches of a stage-piece. *Our hearts are far from each other.*

All these observations apply to the civilized and improving portions of the human race; but they very imperfectly describe the untruthfulness of illiterate nations, where vices are not checked by law, and where the rule of self-preservation is cunning. In attempting to convert the Hindus, our most formidable adversary is hypocrisy. They lock up their heart. We can evoke no true expression of what takes place *there*. When we attempt to raise them, everything seems to give way under us: their honesty supplies no *fulcrum* by which we may move and lift them. The predominance of falsehood is the distinction of Eastern nations and the remoter tribes of the South Seas. Men get further from each other as they recede further from God.

Such is the human race: a family for the most part without truth, each one appearing to the rest other than he is; without confidence, without unity; among whom life, instead of being a fair game upon acknowledged principles of playing, is a trick, a sleight of hand, and stratagem wins the prize. This is a dark picture; but do not misunderstand me. I look upon the world, the large house of God's family; and you, perhaps, are in the midst of a select chamber where hearts are true and friendships staunch: but come with me to less favoured apartments: mingle with men when they mass together. Mark the steps by which they advance in their profession or business; watch them when they confer a favour, when they supplant a rival, when they conclude a bargain; closely observe them in concert, from congresses to cabinets, from parliaments to vestries. Where is the frank attire of natural expression? Where is honest speaking and earnest disinterested work? Rarely indeed shining out from a dark complication of jealousies, overreachings, misunderstandings, and resentments.

Amid this desolate separation of hearts, however, which makes us say in our haste, *all men are liars*, there is one haven in which a man may generally anchor his troubled faith, and where he may rest his aching sight upon unaffected expressions, and his heart upon honest love. It is a happiness, the greatest earth can afford, that after contending with the outside world, wearied by the unceasing vigilance with which we are obliged to walk a path so full of snares, we can retreat to our own home. There at least a man is understood. The glance of his children is genuine. There the caress, the pressure of greeting, is the welcome of a full heart: the smile is no flattery there, the tear no display, the obedience no purchase. There heart comes forth to meet heart; and no longer frozen by the presence of the stranger, they overflow into each other; and amid the music of words that cannot lie, and the brightness of looks that want no construing; amid services that ask no reasons and expect no rewards, a man gives himself up to sweet forgetfulness of care and the dark and stormy world without;

<blockquote>The social hours, swift-winged, unnoticed fleet.</blockquote>

But imagine, if you can, that your home instead of being the asylum of simplicity, innocence, and honest love, were a theatre for dramatic exhibitions; that instead of meeting there with glad and confiding hearts, you were received with parade! Suppose that your very children had an unnatural fear of you, a fear that made them deceitful; that in spite of the fullest revelations of your own heart, they did not, *could not*, understand you! Suppose that you yourself felt a parent's true and passionate regard; you evince it by a tender nurture; but your children, your own children, are unmoved! The kiss of their lips is a show; their little clasp a ceremony. You watch them when they are together, and the merry laugh rings out, and caressses, sympathies and outspoken words, denied to *you*, are exchanged without reserve and without measure; but your presence is a chill; the sound of your voice arrests everything natural; your coming is a sign for artifice; they never answer with an improper word, they run to do your wishes, but it is with a studied alacrity. You give them presents, you impress warm kisses upon them, you indulge and pet them, you use every means to get near their hearts; you want a simple expression addressed to you from *your own child;* your soul yearns for it; be it love, be it anger, anything *real.* But these deceptions kill you! The smile withers, the kiss takes away your breath! you look for your child not in its form, beautifully moulded though that be, but in the heart that closes itself against you. You are worse than childless. For a son, a daughter, upon whose infancy you gazed with the delicious reverie of a parent's newly-enriched heart, for your *children* to unfold the beautiful blossoms of their growth, only to discover the adder of hypocrisy coiled up in the core of their being, hiding a devilish fang beneath the blandishments of a caress! I will not describe the anguish with which a father so stricken and isolated will retire into himself, realizing the bitter words of Job, *They that dwell in my house count me for a stranger: my breath is strange unto my children, for their heart is far from me.*

If ye then, being evil, know what to expect from your children, and shrink from an unnatural picture of childhood without a heart and without truth, how much more shall our heavenly Father be wounded when within the circle of *His* family he receives the honor of the lips only! That He has the views, expectations, and feelings of a parent admits of no doubt, *for the Lord hath spoken, I have nourished and brought up children, and they have rebelled against me. If then I be a father, where is mine honor?* Now God has an outer world, and He has also a place of which He has said, " This is my rest for ever: here will I dwell; for I have desired it." The people of the wide earth know Him not; and when His eye wanders over the millions of heathendom, He expects misunderstanding, coldness, and deceit. His gospel has not been preached, His Spirit has not striven, there. He is grieved and vexed at the stiff-necked nations, and He will in the end draw them unto Himself; but they at present offer Him no retreat, His tabernacle is not among them. He dwells in His church. Here His will is read and honored; His son is acknowledged; His commands obeyed. He loves His house, *beautiful for situation, the joy of the whole earth;* He loves His people; and His joy is to see them walk in the light of His countenance.

But it is here, in His own family, that He utters the lamentation, *Their heart is far from Me!* It is here that he has detected the cheap reverence of a bended knee, and the loathsome incense of unmeaning praise! Consider the wound you inflict upon God the Son, when with what seems to be a penitent glance, you look up, and join in an appeal to His passion and death, while your heart at the very moment is musing far away. He brings you a pure and ardent love; you repay Him with studied gestures, and set phrases of respect. His approach to you is the eager meeting of a Father in haste to be gracious. You draw near with your *mouth* only, and make the interview a jest! You may disclaim an evil purpose; there may be no intention to offer an affront; and were you a stranger in the house, insincerity, or mere speech-reverence would be expected and overlooked; but you say, *Our Father*, without a child's heart! *You*, who look for sincerity in your own children, and, if it were denied you, would be the most inconsolable of mortals! But you think the analogy halts; that the position of our heavenly Father with regard to His children is not precisely similar to yours. If it be not, it is because there are considerations that render the instance of His example infinitely more pathetic and distressing. He has done more for you as a Father, than you can ever do for your own family; His love is stronger, wiser, more lively, more prone to sacrifice, than any parental affection : His right to obedience is more authoritative than any earthly father's claims; and He has a keener a more poignant consciousness of the hurt inflicted by deception, as well as a more intense abhorrence of its wickedness, than you can have. We cannot wonder that among the threatenings of the word of God, the most terrible shaft should be levelled against the hypocrite; that sins of this class should be more hateful to the Holy One than errors of faith or excesses of appetite. *Knowest thou not this of old, since man was placed upon earth, that the joy of the hypocrite is but for a moment?* You will remember that on the two or three occasions during His ministry in which the deeply tranquil spirit of Jesus was flushed for a moment with indignation, showing a spark of *the wrath of the Lamb*, His anger was kindled by the smooth-lipped Pharisee, who carried an asp under his tongue. All classes knew that He was gracious, except the generation of vipers who concealed every species of baseness beneath the folds of a sacred profession. This same Jesus has taught us when we pray, to say, *Our Father!* Let us never again repeat it with a cold and distant heart. Sincerity is obviously the first law of prayer. Let us, in the words of Jeremiah, lift up our *heart* with our hands unto God in the heavens. And in ways as well as in words let there be warmth, transparency, and love. Our spirits are ever liable to withdraw from the form of duty, leaving it a dead work; but let us check this tendency to lifelessness by *looking unto Jesus*, whose inspiration shall pervade, sanctify, and prosper all our service.

SERMON XV.

Rev. iii. 14, 15, 16.

"And unto the angel of the church of the Laodiceans write: These things saith the Amen, the faithful and true witness, the beginning of the creation of God; I know thy works that thou art neither cold nor hot: I would thou wert cold or hot. So then because thou art lukewarm, and neither cold nor hot, I will spue thee out of my mouth."

You will have learned from the lesson that this is the language of Jesus Christ to one of the seven churches. You will be able to recall the circumstance that each of the seven epistles addressed to them, is prefaced by an enunciation of some of the titles and distinctions that naturally designate or properly reward the Captain of our Salvation. To the church at Pergamos He is *the avenger of wrong,* grasping the two-edged sword. To the church at Thyatira which had been nearly devoured by the hypocrisy and seductions of Jezebel, He subscribes Himself, *the Son of God, with eyes like unto a flaming fire,* penetrating and consuming saintly profession, shooting to the reins of the heart, bringing everything to light and to proof. You may perceive that these and similar titles in the salutation of each epistle, indicate the character of the message transmitted. It is remarkably so in the letter to the Laodicean Christians. Against this church, the Lord is about to utter a deep complaint of wrong done to Himself; of that species of offence which men, in dread of the infamy attached to it, are most careful to avoid, the violation of oaths, the perjury of the heart: He was about to charge His own people, the children of light, with deeds which the children of this world brand as a reproach to our nature. He opens the accusation therefore with an appropriate and impressive solemnity. *These things saith the Amen, the faithful and true witness, the beginning of the creation of God.* The two first titles explain each other. *Amen* signifies *true, faithful, certain.* The Lord bears His testimony against the offending church as the Amen Witness. His words are not the hasty expressions of resentment, nor the perverted representation of prejudice; they convey the truth explicitly and simply. The Laodiceans may not readily admit the charge, may not be conscious of the guilt; but every accent of that charge is pronounced with an *Amen*; and it is the Amen of God Himself. " The beginning of the creation of

God," is a divine title,—*the Origin of the creation*, whose mind is the mirror in which all truth is at once reflected. *Let God be true and every man a liar. He is justified when He speaketh, and clear when He judgeth.*

We have now to consider that part of the Laodicean letter which contains a complaint, and a threatening.

I. *I know thy works that thou art neither cold nor hot: I would thou wert cold or hot.*

These words derive their force from a peculiar covenant under which Christ and the Laodiceans were united. It was a bond surpassing in tenderness and in sacramental authority the holiest and closest earthly fellowship. The union between Christ and His disciple is composed of every element that can bind two persons together, and possesses these elements in an infinitely perfect degree. It comprehends the indentures of servitude, the covenants of friendship, the blood of family, and the mysterious betrothment of marriage; everything that is ardent in passion, authoritative in obligation, and binding in law. Passing over that exquisite drama of love, Solomon's Song, where the doubts, the dejections, and the extacies of that passion are painted with a fidelity that gives it the highest place among this class of compositions, let me select from Hosea,* an avowal of Christ's attachment to the believer, "I will betroth thee unto me for ever; yea I will betroth thee unto me in righteousness, and in judgment, and in lovingkindness, and in mercies." Here is a similar disclosure from Jeremiah,† "I have loved thee with an everlasting love: therefore with lovingkindness have I drawn thee." Such was the plighted vow and the fervid declaration of Jesus to the Laodicean believers; and they had professed to return the passion, "We love Him because He hath first loved us. Thy vows O God are upon us. What shall we render unto the Lord for all His benefits towards us? Our soul thirsteth for Thee, our soul followeth hard after Thee. Set us as a seal upon Thine heart, as a seal upon Thine arm: for love is strong as death; many waters cannot quench it." In burning words like these, had the Laodicean church described the kindling of their own love for Jesus.

But this is not all. We cannot know the sacramental engagements that bind the believer to Christ unless we consider the manner in which they were brought together. You will find an account of it condensed in the words, "He first loved us." He who com-

* Chap. ii. 19.   . † Chap. xxxi. 3.

plains of the Laodiceans was the first to love them. It was not the love of an equal, that brought with it no authority and left no debt; it yearned for an object infinitely below it; it took the form of mercy and self-sacrifice, of strenuous and costly labour, of every species of humiliation and suffering; it surrendered life itself to win its purpose. The Laodiceans went not after Christ; Christ went after them: He found the shadow of death upon them: He descended into that shadow and saw them lying, insensible and helpless, within the grasp of the grim destroyer who "had the power of death." No eye pitied them save His, no arm but His could attempt salvation. They were His creatures; had been convicted for treason against Himself; it was not innocent misery that He pitied, it was not to rescue virtue from captivity, or to vindicate innocence from calumny, that He armed Himself for deeds of mercy: the souls He loved were *wicked, depraved,* and *righteously lost.* He would bless them that had cursed Him, He would do good to them that had hated Him, He would pray for them that had despitefully used Him. This was the spirit in which Jesus followed the Laodiceans,—prepared to save them; to put forth all the power of God to justify the law that had condemned them, and to give scope to the mercy that impatiently waited to begin her work. There lay a road impassable to all but Himself between Jesus and lost souls. It was a road of tears and blood; it led Him through valleys of shame and over mountains of labour; it exposed Him to the contradictions of sinners, to the darker assaults of demons, the furies that hell sends out to dog the steps of the sinner; and it brought Him to the last anguish of humanity, *death.* But no toil exhausted Him, no terror chilled his resolution, no impediment shook the purpose of His heart. Lost souls lay at the end of His career, and he staid not, until, with *vesture dipped in blood,* He reached them, *mighty to save ;* and he did save them : saved these Laodiceans from the ever-blazing furnace of God's wrath : lifted each soul into His arms, washed it in His blood, gave it a new nature, a new dress, and a new name; entered its title to heaven in the Book of Life; and the recompense He sought was love : not gratitude for condescension; this was too formal, too cold for Him; He demanded *love for love ;* not merely a subject's homage, but a brother's heart, a child's trust, the fond devotion of a friend, passing the love of women ! Less than this would be a satire upon *Gethsemane* and *Calvary ;* it would be a fouler wrong than the mock coronation with which Herod derided the majesty of the Saviour. A crown of thorns from an enemy is better than a cold heart from a friend. The reciprocal sentiment of a soul saved from hell, must be *love;* love in the highest ardour of its passion, absorbing all lower attachments, and inspiring all other pursuits. If you think these expressions are too strong, look into the New Testament; there I find them warranted by command and proved by experience: *The love of Christ constraineth me. Thou shalt love the Lord with all thy heart. I bow my knees unto the Father of our Lord Jesus Christ,—that Christ may dwell in your hearts by faith: that ye, being rooted and grounded in love, may be able to comprehend with all saints what is the breadth, and length, and depth, and height; and to know the love of Christ, which passeth knowledge, that ye might be filled with all the fulness of God. As the Father hath loved me, so have I loved you: continue ye in my love.* Love is the spring of the believer's union with Christ; his service and his joy flow from it; it is the grand distinction of his discipleship.

The Laodicean believers had allowed this distinction to die out! This was the complaint. They had no *love* for Jesus. They still observed the formalities of worship; still baptized in His name, attended the ministry of His servants, and decently maintained the ornaments of religion: but He tried their reins; He looked not at the prostrate knee and the uplifted hand; He searched the *heart* of that Laodicean assembly; He found to His deep grief that He was forgotten *there;* He had no place in their *hearts,*—HE, who was Himself all heart; who had shed His blood to save them from death; whose life had been the price of their rescue,—souls whom He had betrothed for ever; His by creative right, by redemptionary purchase, by covenant oath, and by love sacramentally pledged; whose names were engraven on His hands, and treasured in His heart. No love for Jesus from *these* souls! *I know their works*, He writes, in bitter words, " and I know that they love Me not! They are not hostile to Me, they do not blaspheme My name, pollute My Sabbaths, and throw down My altars. But what to Me is an altar, unless it be kindled with love? Better it were thrown down! What to Me is a frigid Sabbath, and the calling of an assembly without heart? What to Me is the spreading forth of hands, unless the spirit be bowed? What to Me is the homage of gesture and voice? Better a heathen festival, than a formal Sabbath; better the cabalistic mantrams of idol-

P

atry, than hypocritical invocations to the true Saviour. *I know thy works that thou art neither cold nor hot ; I would thou wert cold or hot.*" Christ had enemies in Laodicea; they did what they professed to do; they hated Him, they fought against Him; they were naturally and necessarily at enmity with Him. He had never touched their hearts, and called them His love and His bride. He expected to be crucified by *these*. But what were His friends doing? Taking care of themselves; doing as much for the Lord as their safety and honor permitted; avoiding extremes to escape unpleasant notice. They had families to bring up, business to look after, and a civil position to maintain. O brethren! to accept Jesus upon conditions! Did He take care of Himself when He went forth to serve *them?* Was He judicious enough to avoid extremes? He was the Son of God; did He look after His reputation? When Peter advised Him to be temperate and neutral, He replied with holy indignation, Get thee behind me Satan, thou art an offence unto Me. It behoves Christ to suffer. For their sakes I sanctify Myself. Christ abhors neutrality. For His sake *we* must sanctify ourselves, placing ourselves at His feet for time and for eternity; to live as He shall choose, to acknowledge but one Lord, to know but one service, to love but one object, to do all this in *extremes*, that is, with all our heart, mind, soul, and strength.

I hope you have not failed to apply these observations. Christ writes a letter to you, and He bids me read it. *These things saith the Amen, the faithful, and true witness, the beginning of the creation of God; I know thy works that thou art neither cold nor hot: I would thou wert cold or hot.* Is not this part of the letter an exact description of us? Where are they who have lost their first love, and are now living at ease in Zion? Did you in the days of your espousals love Christ too ardently? Did you at that time allow Him too distinguished a place in your hearts, and devote to His service an improper proportion of your time? Have you been happier since the ardour of your early piety abated? You are more cautious now than you were then. You never used to miss an opportunity of speaking for Him, of bringing honor to His name, and sacrifices to His cause. Now you imagine you have less time to give to these things; your attention is engaged and divided by a wider range of interests. And is it well, think you, that this is so? Do you live better, work better, suffer better, and can you die better, than you could have done then? You execrate those who violate the marriage vow; you censure the prodigal who despises the filial bond; you scorn the man who puts a lie into his right hand before he grasps yours, and under the mask of friendship attempts to injure you; you justify the hanging of a conspirator and the infamy that cleaves to his house. *What has become of your own marriage-vow to Christ, solemnly exchanged at the Cross and ratified by blood?* Your adulterous heart has gone after other lords, and Jesus, your rightful husband stands before you with a dishonoured name! *Where is your filial bond?* You have rebelled against the authority of your Father's house: from disrespectful and dishonourable motives you have left your home and are now a wanderer without support and without decency. *Where is the warmth and fidelity of your former friendship?* You put a hand in Christ's, exclaiming,

> O happy day that fixed my choice
> On Thee my Saviour and my God;
> Well may this glowing heart rejoice,
> And tell its raptures all abroad.

What says the glowing heart now? I will tell you what Christ says of it. "He setteth up his idols in his heart, and putteth the stumbling block of his iniquity before his face. His foolishness perverteth his way, and his heart fretteth against the Lord." *What has become of your loyalty to the Prince who forgave your first treason and whom in the instance of that gracious clemency you swore never again to offend?* You remember the promise, "I will extol Thee, my God, O King, and I will bless Thy name for ever and ever: every day will I bless Thee." Are you blessing Him to-day? You say you are not His enemies. Then why lounge outside the King's camp, without equipment or position, indifferent to the marshalling of His hosts and the trump of battle?

II. *Because thou art lukewarm, and neither cold nor hot, I will spue thee out of my mouth.*

I need not explain that there is here an allusion to the nauseous effects of drinking tepid water. It is the strongest language of *disgust* and *loathing*. I need not tell you that words of this kind were very rarely spoken by Christ. On two or three occasions only did the wrath of the Lamb explode in a *threat*. He never answered His revilers; He pitied and forgave those whom a censorious world had judged to be beyond forgiveness; many upon whom He wrought the most signal mercies were notoriously immoral; and He prayed for His murderers. The habitual temper of His spirit was, and is, patient endurance and forgiveness of injuries. When sinners had placed themselves beyond the possibility of redemption, He wept over them. If His mind was not always happy like the sunshine, its clouded sorrows concealed no thunder; they were "big with mercies," and broke in blessings upon the head of His enemies. It was an extraordinary provocation indeed that made *Him* angry; and the offence that most sensibly wounded the holy Saviour was hypocrisy. The sanctimonious iniquity of the Pharisees, the affected candour of the scribes, incurred His heaviest rebukes. But in no passage, save the text, do I recollect an expression of *loathing*, the most emphatic species of dislike of which we are capable. It is the most painful and incurable temper of mind that any object can awaken in us. We can pacify anger, we can conquer repugnance, we may moderate every species of aversion, save loathing. It is a feeling over which the will has no power. It is as if our whole nature were involuntarily ejecting the offensive object. It is not whether we consent to accept it, we *cannot*—our senses, tastes, and nerves, throw it from us. Just as in the body a poisonous substance is rejected by a spasmodic action of the stomach, so we cast from us whatever grossly offends our moral nature. There are many persons whom we dislike, there are some who move our indignation; but there is hardly one whose qualities are so repulsive as to excite loathing. These observations may serve to exhibit the image of the text in relief, and to indicate Christ's abhorrence of the lukewarm Christian. Strange conjunction of words, *lukewarm Christian!*

The first thing that strikes us is the wonderful revolution of temper from liking to loathing. Is it possible for Christ to loath what He once loved? If there be any meaning in the text, it is possible. How came the Laodiceans to be lukewarm? Did the temperature of their love start from heat or cold? Heat undoubtedly: it was a descending, a cooling piety; love waxing cold, zeal burning low, life going out: implying a disunion of heart, a criminal infidelity of affection, a displacement of confidence, a breaking of solemn faith, a base dishonor upon all previous expressions and tokens of love. When our affections have been devoted to an object, and have commanded and obtained the relinquishment of every other interest; when everything has gone with them, property, name, reputation, intellect, heart, and life itself; when we feel that we have kept back nothing; when we have made a sacrifice of our whole selves without question or grudge;—then if we meet with an insufficient or an ill-sustained response, we are shocked; but recovering, we welcome the first explanation that offers itself; for the heart that loves wholly is not quick to suspect; but if the explanation come not, and proof after proof, in ruthless demonstration, tell us that our love is not returned, our trust is not esteemed, our great sacrifice is simply permitted, then love changes into loathing: you feel how mean, how unworthy, how innately repulsive must that nature be that could be unfaithful to an affection like yours; and this would be the natural expression of your disgust, "I will spue thee out of my mouth." But this illustration only half explains the problem before us. We can have no conception of the love of Christ, or the sacrifices it made to carry out its purposes; hence we can know as little of the wrongs which those inflict upon Him who allow their love to grow cold, and their union to become formal and distant. But the threatening will not on this account lose its force. It implies all that we can understand by it, and dread from it; and probably, as much more, as a Divine affection surpasses the imperfect analogy in our own mind by which we seek to understand it. *Thou hast left thy first love. Remember therefore from whence thou art fallen, and repent, and do the first works. He that hath an ear, let him hear what the Spirit saith unto the churches.*

SERMON XVI.

1 KINGS xix. 11, 12, 13.

"And he said, Go forth, and stand upon the mount before the Lord. And, behold, the Lord passed by, and a great and strong wind rent the mountains, and brake in pieces the rocks before the Lord; but the Lord was not in the wind: and after the wind an earthquake; but the Lord was not in the earthquake: And after the earthquake a fire; but the Lord was not in the fire: and after the fire a still small voice. And it was so, when Elijah heard it, that he wrapped his face in his mantle, and went out, and stood in the entering in of the cave."

ELIJAH is the most remarkable prophet of Old Testament history. His introduction and exit have a wild abruptness and obscurity that rather befit a hero of romance than an historic personage. He comes upon the epoch of his career full armed, is the leader of a few prodigious events, and escapes in a whirlwind. He was probably born in Thisbe, a city of Galilee; but as he is said to have been of the inhabitants of Gilead, it may be supposed that he had sojourned a long time in that country.

His parentage, his rank, his private calling, we are not permitted even to conjecture. It is not unlikely that for many years he had been a man of study and prayer. A character like his, of so much energy and presence when brought into action, often acquires its great features in retirement. Moses had a training of forty years before he was qualified to be the founder and lawgiver of a great people: John the Baptist spent his youth in deserts, where deep meditation and holy converse with God gave to the voice of the wilderness the tone that startled a nation; and Elijah who occupies a middle space between these illustrious lights, and, like them, burst upon his age with a sudden splendour, must have had a long and careful preparation for the mission he was destined to fulfil.

Elijah began his work when the fear and even the worship of God had died out in Israel. The people since Solomon's death had been growing worse and worse. Their present reigning prince, Ahab, did evil in the sight of the Lord above all that were before him. As a stroke of defiance against Jehovah, as well as in contempt of all decency, he had married into a heathen family; an alliance that brought frightful disasters upon the cause of God; for Jezebel was one of the fiercest and most abandoned women of her time. She was bent upon making all her lord's subjects *pagans;* she carried her father's gods and her father's priests into the land of Israel, erected temples to Baal, and pressed upon her husband the necessity of getting rid of the prophets of Jehovah. A bloody persecution was then opened upon the Lord's anointed; hundreds of holy men were butchered because they refused to bend the knee to Baal; and every warning voice was silenced in death or in captivity. It was at this crisis, when the altars of idolatry covered the land, and when nearly a thousand foreign priests, of a foreign religion, rode over the consciences and spoiled the substance of the people, that the prophet Elijah appeared. The blood of his brethren, visible in every public resort and highway, told him there was but a step between *him* and death: he walked on the ashes of martyrdom, and over his head there hung the sword of the persecutor. These circumstances gave an iron rigour to his principles, a certain gloomy strength to his character, and a stern severity to his discourses. The message he was commanded to deliver to Israel, and to Ahab in particular, accorded with and strengthened these features of his mind. He belonged to a class of ministers who speak threatenings and administer judgments; and the iniquity he saw in high places, the idolatry and sacrilege that polluted the country, impressed the prophet with the justice of those awful visitations of which he was the agent.

The ministry of Elijah, which was that of a destroying angel, is intended to teach us the inefficacy of judgments as a converting instrumentality. The prophet had become depressed because sword, pestilence, and famine, had failed to scourge a rebellious people to a right mind. During a three years' drought, he watched the effect of starvation. He had foretold that this judgment would chastise the monarch and his people for their crimes. The famine came with terrible and wide-spreading calamity; and Elijah went into the solitudes of Samaria to await its results upon the public mind of Israel. His giant soul was revolving in its depths the sufferings, the humiliations, the ultimate submission, of a backsliding and reprobate people. Let us follow the prophet to Samaria, and abide with him there, until his reappearance before Ahab, when the famine shall have done its work. God is about to read him exquisite lessons on tenderness; for he had known little else than the terrors of the Lord. The Divine voice drew him to a brook near the Jordan, and there the stern man was softened by the ministry of a bird. When we have become harsh and austere in our ways by a long familiarity with the hypocrisy and injustice of our fellow-men, nothing so quickly touches a spring of tenderness as the instinctive attachment or offices of some inferior creature. Receiving his daily bread from the beak of a raven, he must have felt that providence was as gentle as it was terrible: and that perhaps *love* was "mightiest in the mightiest." He remained here until, for want of rain, the stream of his hiding place dried up: the Lord then commanded him to journey northward, to Zarephath, a large inland village, lying between Tyre and Sidon, where a poor widow had been appointed to sustain him. There were many widows in *Israel;* why was he sent to a *heathen* woman of Sidon? To teach him, what perhaps he never knew before, that there were sheep which were not of his fold. The conduct of Jezebel had probably increased his national emnity against all Gentiles. He supposed that Jehovah could have no mercy on the accursed votaries of Baal; and yet Baal was one of the principal gods of Sidon, and the woman to whom he was the preacher of mercy and salvation was a worshipper of that idol. Arriving at the village he found that the famine had preceded him; the poor widow's means had been so pinched by the dearth that the last handful of meal was in the barrel and the last drop of oil in the cruse. But the oil and the meal wasted not while the man of God was with her. The miracle of the unfailing meal, however, like the miracle of the five loaves, did not convert those for whose sake it was wrought. Whether Elijah during the twelve months he spent with this Sarepta family, directly instructed them in the knowledge of the true God, we know not; but the woman appears to have remained a stranger to the truth until the Lord afflicted her with the death of her child. It was the sickness of her daughter that drove the Canaanitish woman to Christ. It was the death of her son that bowed the woman of Sarepta to the confession of Jehovah. The prophet took from the mother's bosom the corpse of her boy and carried him up-stairs into the loft where he slept. She overheard the breathing of those mighty prayers that brought back the soul of the child; and when he was restored to her arms once more, the living son of her heart, she exclaimed, "Now by this I know that thou art a man of God, and that the word of the Lord in thy mouth is truth."

But Elijah must leave Sarepta for Samaria. The three years' famine was now closing, and the Lord commanded the prophet to show himself unto Ahab, to make another appeal and another stand for Jehovah. It was to be supposed that the people, subdued and crushed by a long affliction, would now yield to any demonstration that might contrast the power of the Lord with the impostures of Baal. Elijah met the king : and after upbraiding him with a sharpness and authority which no kingly presence could resist, he called upon Ahab to decide the controversy that now divided and was destroying the country. A famine had reigned for three years. Had Baal sent it, or was it the scourge of Jehovah? Rain was yet denied; it was the duty of the king and his people to humble themselves before the deity who had punished them, whether Jehovah or Baal. A trial of the gods was proclaimed. Elijah proposed that the witnesses should assemble on Mount Carmel, a neighbouring promontory about two thousand feet high, stretching into the Mediterranean sea. The king's decree summoned the priests of Baal, to meet Jehovah's prophet on Carmel's top; and all the people were commanded to accompany them. There stands the Tishbite, alone, worn down with care, and travelling, and watching; but his eye sparkles with the indignation of jealousy, and with an expression of ominous irony. There, on the side of idolatry, stand in imposing array the flower of Baal's priesthood, four hundred and fifty men, with their divinations and enchantments. I need not detail the triumphs of that glorious day, when in the sight of Israel and Israel's king, the pretensions of the god of Ekron were stripped off; when the priests of Jezebel, smarting under the caustic banter of the prophet, danced round their altars with frantic mortification, crying to a god that could not save; and when the God of heaven descended in fiery rebuke, consuming the sacrifice of Elijah and the indecision of the people! Now, thought the prophet, if we can follow up this splendid testimony by putting every heathen priest to the sword, we shall annihilate idolatry at a blow! Resistless for the moment, he gave thé command, and the people, eager to show the sincerity of their repentance, arrested the priests of Jezebel, brought them down to the brook Kishon and slew them there. To crown the triumphs of this day, the rain began to fall; and now there seemed to be nothing wanting that miracle could do to complete the conversion of the people. Elijah hastened first to the court to find the queen overwhelmed with defeat and humiliation; but Jezebel, so far from being terrified into conviction by the appalling wonders of Carmel, was preparing to take his life!

This was so heavy and sudden a blow to Elijah's faith in the converting power of judgments, that courage and dignity forsook him for a time, and he fled like a frighted deer because a woman had threatened him! An angel of God found him in a wilderness of Beersheba, lying under a juniper tree; bitterly complaining of his lot and praying the Lord to take his life. It was now that Jehovah explained to his servant by the impressive signs described in the text, that power might avenge and destroy, but could not *win;* that the silent intellectual process of instruction and spiritual influence can alone reach the heart and change the man.

The theatre of these signs was *Horeb,* celebrated of old for displays of the Divine terrors. Here Moses saw the flaming majesty of the I AM in the bush. Here was Sinai, the mount that might be touched; that burned with fire, and trembled when the trump of God gave forth the voice of words. Recalling these events, and impressed by these associations, Elijah, after a journey of forty days, drew near to this Horeb, the mount of God; and entering a cave or grot, hollowed out in one of its sides, he lodged there. Here God found him.

"What dost thou here Elijah?" The prophet answered in a distempered mood, that he had been jealous for the Lord of Hosts: that in spite of all he had done to reclaim Israel, the divine covenants were yet broken, the altars profaned, the prophets slain, and himself, the sole remaining witness for the truth, they were seeking to destroy. Then the Lord commanded the melancholy and despairing Seer to ascend to the top of the mount; and while he stood there, surrounded by bleak and barren hills, fit images of power and desolation, the Lord passed by in a succession of grand and suggestive phenomena. There were four signs; of which three were *material*, and the fourth *intellectual*.

1. A strong wind swept by, rending the imbedded cliffs of Horeb and scattering them like stubble. The stormy soul of Elijah found a congenial element in this untamed and mighty agent; and he perhaps wished he could ride upon its wings, turn its head toward Samaria, and demolish the usurpation of Baal. But while he watched for some particular appearance to indicate the presence of Jehovah; some strange glory or voice to show that the hurricane was a fit chariot for the career of a God, the storm fell; and the prophet knew that *the Lord was not in the wind.*

2. Then followed another sign, more terrific than a tempest. Perhaps in all nature there is nothing which so nearly resembles what we should think to be the immediate interposition of God as an *earthquake*. "After the wind, an earthquake." As the prophet felt that ancient and lofty pile of hills, apparently immortal in their stedfastness, give way beneath his feet, writhing helplessly in the grasp of some unseen power, like a convulsed child, he must have thought, " Surely God is *here !* These fearful shakings and hurlings are the tokens of His dread presence:" and he might have repeated to himself the triumphant chant of a psalm he had often sung, What ails ye, ye mountains, that ye skip like rams; and ye little hills like lambs? Tremble, thou earth, at the presence of the Lord, at the presence of the God of Jacob! But *the Lord was not in the earthquake ;* the convulsions subsided without a sign.

3. The third wonder that passed before the eye of the now perplexed prophet, was an element as destructive as an earthquake but far more imposing. Shining about the brightness of the sun, roaring and consuming, a huge fire played about the rocks on which Elijah stood. And as he saw its nimble tongues of flame lick up the hard verdure of

the ground, and split and melt the rocks with its devouring heat, he knew that this fierce brightness had been from the beginning a chosen vehicle of Jehovah. He remembered Sodom and Gomorrah; he remembered Sinai, part of the very hill that now blazed around him, when lightnings had accompanied the declaration of law; and he probably waited to receive from that fire another commandment for Israel. There stood the stern man, in the midst of devastation. The wind had shaken, the earthquake had swallowed up, the fire had consumed; but God had not spoken! The prophet had been awed, but not *instructed*. He had gone up to the mount doubtful, dissatisfied, perhaps self-condemned: the material signs gave him no relief. They were splendid and dreadful, but there was no *mind* in them.

4. While he thus stood bewildered, debating with himself what this might mean, the last sign explained all: it was a *still small voice:* it was still, because no sound struck audibly on the ear; it was small, because no ostentatious medium conveyed it; it was the voice of *mind* whispering to mind. God spake to Elijah; and without any symbol there were thoughts interchanged that bowed the prophet's soul to the dust. And it came to pass when Elijah heard it, or felt it, he wrapped

his face in his mantle and returned to his cave, standing in the entrance to hear the voice again, as if repeating the words of Samuel, *Speak, Lord, for thy servant heareth.*

My dear brethren, that which bows the mind, that which makes a man wrap his face in his mantle in silent and intelligent reverence, is not a sign that strikes upon the senses, but a thought understood and felt in the heart. Miracles have an historic value, but they have seldom produced in those who witnessed them a moral benefit; neither error nor vice can spring from a miracle, nor can either be ejected by a miracle: they arise from the connexion of mind with mind, and must be destroyed by a new mental fellowship.

This will be manifest if we follow the course of the Divine revelation. The patriarchs transmitted a few simple and fixed beliefs; the Jewish economy dispensed miracles and types; the knowledge of God became more defined and enlarged; it was systematized in laws, but national and local in its application. When Christ came, He made the gospel the subject and instrument of teaching, fulfilling the prediction, *And they shall be all taught of God.* Divine knowledge, in coming down to us from the past, has become more and more a voice speaking to the heart; more and more free from material mediums. When Abraham embraced the knowledge of God it was on its way to *us;* when Moses lodged it in the Jewish tabernacle it was purifying itself for us; when Christ found it there and baptized it with the Holy Ghost and with fire, He sent it forth to us. It is now doing its greatest work, not by flood and fire, although there are cities in the world as wicked as Sodom; not by miracles, although there is as hard a scepticism as ever reigned in Judea or Rome; but by the *still small voice* of instruction, supported and carried out to gracious results by the silent communion of the Holy Ghost.

These are the last and crowning means of Christianity. Everything else, by whatever name you call it, belongs to the three first signs. And what a fondness we have for these signs, the picturesque and the striking! But what do they gain who seek to embellish the church with a gorgeous architecture; who cultivate the sublimity of domes and capitals; who subdue by a solemn coloring the very light that falls upon the worshippers; who place in imposing situations the picture, the statue, the emblem; who burnish their altars with gold, and bring to the holy crucifix the homage of tapers and the genuflexions of surplice and mitre; who enter the assembly with the music of chanted litanies, and terrify the people by the thunder of anathemas? The Lord is not in the architecture, the picture, the music, the pomp: you see no more here than the three signs of the prophet; you must seek the Lord in the voice of the conscience: this is the sign of the gospel dispensation, the word, and not the picture; Christ, and not the crucifix; the Holy Ghost, and not the seven candles. If we stop with the three signs, we go no further than the heathen. The negro falls down before the whirlwind and the earthquake, and cries, Lo God is here! The Parsee worships the shining fire. But their impressions are sensuous and temporary; fading before the heart is touched, for the still small voice of instruction is wanting. Look at the people around us! We see whole nations prostrate before the three signs. To the Hindu the splendours of Hinduism are the whirlwind, the earthquake, and the fire; and his homage is fear and admiration. When I have seen an idol arrayed in traditionary terrors, and magnificently paraded through the streets of a large native town, and in the night too; and when ten thousand human beings have pressed near to worship amid the gleaming of innumerable torches of colored light, and rockets and candles of every device shooting up into the air; and when the priests have sung in solemn cadence, and the multitudes have shouted their acclamations, I have caught the prevailing awe. With all my better knowledge I could not resist the terror and beauty of the spectacle; *but the Lord was not there.* The multitudes returned to their homes with an intoxicated sense and a fevered imagination; but no silent voice to instruct and win them to God. But I have taken one of those Hindus whom the earthquake and the fire had dazzled but not changed; I have drawn him away from the three signs, and invited him to wait with me for the fourth; and while we listened, a still small voice spoke in our hearts; and when he heard it, he wrapped his face in his mantle and cried, *What must I do to be saved!* And the effect of that voice was a new heart and a new life. It was the silent winning of Calvary, and not the fiery testimony of Carmel: it was not Moses or Elijah thundering forth the law upon the senses, but Jesus breathing truth and grace into the soul.

Let me persuade those who are conscious of it to take heed to the whisper of God. See that ye refuse not Him that speaketh: for if they escaped not that refused Elijah, who spake on earth, *much more shall not we escape if we turn away from Him that speaketh from heaven.* Have you ever bowed before this voice and hidden your face in penitence? Perhaps amidst the clamour and discord of louder voices, the still accents of Jesus escaped you. He that hath ears to hear let him hear. We cannot catch the sound without profound listening. When we do hear it, speaking pardon from the Cross, speaking help from the right hand of God, speaking victory in the conflict,

>'Tis music in the sinner's ear,
>'Tis life and health and peace.

For the comfort of those who have been terrified by the storm and fire of the law, I am commanded to promise that the blessed sign of a Saviour's presence shall follow. You have been convinced of sin; have quaked beneath the threatenings of Horeb; a storm of distemper and doubt is rending your souls; but follow Elijah's example; wait, be of good courage, and He shall strengthen your heart; the thick cloud of sin shall pass away before the still small voice of heavenly peace.

SERMON XVII.

LUKE x. 42.

" But one thing is needful: and Mary hath chosen that good part, which shall not be taken away from her."

WHICH is the *good* part? is the grand question of life. It is not possible to divide the application of life's energies between a number of great objects: for although the capriciousness of our tastes, and the interfering claims of corresponding attractions, may induce us to attempt the possession and enjoyment of them *all*, it will be found that every man's life will be one thing; that whether he intend it or not, it will be a single career, wherein the diversities of pursuit and of vicissitude will be but the inequalities of one grand trunk-road to heaven or hell. He may not be aware that his life is of any importance—there may be nothing to distinguish it from the common level of social existence; it may be apparently useless, obscure, unknown; but it is about to leap into the gulf of outer darkness, or to mingle with, and lose itself in, a sea of light. What moment must attach to the leading principles of that life! By leading principles I mean those first feelings and decisions which determine us to take the right hand road instead of the left, or the left instead of the right. Every one of you is on a journey, and every traveller is in one of these roads. There may be slight deviations in your steps; the man in the left hand road may in the course of his walking swerve to the right side of it. This may retard his progress, but it does not affect the direction of his path. You may have good desires to-day and bad desires to-morrow; you may be a pattern of virtue this hour and a warning to virtue the next; but the question is, in which road are you walking? I wish to press upon my young friends the fact that whether they have made up their minds or no, as to the path or the portion they shall choose, they are walking a path, and spending a portion. In religious matters, to say, "I am waiting, I have not made up my mind," is folly; as much so as it would be in a passenger by railway, who should say that he was hesitating about the road he should take, when he is speeding on in a definite line at the rate of thirty miles an hour. We have the power to select and to adhere to what we choose; but we are moving none the less if we make no choice at all; and in the end, God will make us strictly accountable for the issue of the journey. I feel anxious to secure the attention of the young, because they have no established convictions, and their minds are easily turned. I want to secure an early decision for the narrow way and the good part. *I am the way*, and *I am the bread of life*. Here is the path and the portion. If I had the ability to present Christ to you in the beauty and grandeur of his nature and in the tender affectionateness of his character, you would at once perceive that you were made to love no other, to admire no other; to confide in, and live with no other. Your connection with earthly objects, your transactions with them, your pleasure in them, your dependence on them, would be so trifling in comparison with your fellowship with Him, that you would only reckon them at all for His sake; and their power to delight or benefit you would be His gift, and they would be several ways of enjoying *Him*. But we are slow to apprehend a comeliness which gratifies no external sense of beauty. There is nothing in the face of the *Man of sorrows* which would invite a second glance from a worldly eye. I have seen thousands from the gay world crowd the saloons of art to look upon the painted Christ of some great master, whose exquisite pencil had traced with startling fidelity a face of suffering, meekness and love, and with the magic of color and tint had wrought a soul into the canvas: but the language of admiration was not, "Come see if there ever was sorrow like this," but, "See if there ever was *painting like this.*" The sermons of Italian art impress the fancy and give a pensive hue to the imagination, but they never touch the conscience. It may be thought a gothic remark, but the artist has misjudged his province when he attempts to give us patterns of things in the heavens.

Less comely still to the worldly man is the religion of Christ; for its symbol is a standard of dishonor. The doctrines of the Cross enjoin absolute separation from all that the carnal mind holds to be desirable and precious. Christianity puts a mean value upon houses and lands, upon distinctions and honors. If you compare its vocabulary with that of the world you will find that the same words stand for totally opposite ideas. Thus, the word *darkness* in one, means *light* in the other; the word *foolishness* in one, means *wisdom* in the other; the word *god* in one, means *devil* in the other, and so on. It is true that this hostility in taste and phraseology is not so manifest now as in earlier times when the confession of Christ was unfashionable; but the applauded toleration of the present day is only granted to the externalism of piety. The religion of the heart is as objectionable as ever to the unconverted man. You may talk about the church of Christ, discuss the character of its ministers, the wisdom of its institutions, the inconsistencies of its professors; but you must not speak to an individual about the necessity of his own conversion. And there is a mutual understanding between professing Christians on this subject, so that one knows, as by instinct, how far it is prudent for him to go in conversing on religion. "The carnal mind is enmity against God, and is not subject to the law of God, neither indeed can be." It therefore only remains for me to pray that while I exhibit the excellencies and person of the despised Son of God, the Holy Spirit may give you an eye to appreciate and a heart to admire, love, and choose, like Mary, the *chiefest among ten thousand—the altogether lovely*.

There is nothing in the New Testament narratives so full of touching and instructive incident as the connection of Jesus with a Bethany family, a brother and two sisters. "Now Jesus loved Martha and her sister and Lazarus." When passing through the village on His way to Jerusalem He made their house His home. And as they lived but two miles from the city, He used after the day's labour, to return to Bethany in the evening, spend the night there, and walk back to the city the next morning. He sometimes took several of His disciples with him, for the family were in good circumstances, and able to accommodate not only their illustrious guest, but his friends. The sisters were types of distinct phases of life. Martha was busy with her hands, Mary with her thoughts; Martha laboured, and Mary listened. It is remarkable that persons of one family and one training should be so variously moulded. But although I am tempted to continue the comparison of these two daughters of Abraham as models of two representative features of Christian mind, the ideal and the practical, both equally essential, though both finding fault with each other, I must defer it for another occasion, and consider Mary by herself, as an illustration of what has been already advanced, that in respect of the design and end of life, we can have but one part, and but one way—and Mary chose the *good* part. The word *part* signifies the share of an inheritance. Mary had recently found it at Jesus' feet, and was overcome by the new and strange feelings which the love of God had awakened in her heart. Her thoughtful nature gave itself up to the wonderful revelations of the lips upon which she hung; and her sister, who perceived the change, though she understood it not, imputed the rapt attention and fixed eye of Mary to the enthusiasm of a gratified listener, whereas they betokened the new and transporting fellowship into which a soul enters when it first believes in Jesus. Mary had been wont to help her sister; strangely did she now seem to neglect her duty. Every duty of life is not only compatible with piety, but derives from it its safest counsels and its highest inspiration. But when we first close our eyes upon the world and open them upon heaven, the darkness we leave and the light we find, the dungeon we escape from, and the free holiday air into which we come, and for the first time breathe and live, the guilt which made us afraid of God, and the forgiveness which makes us cry Abba, Father! are states of position, knowledge, and feeling, so violently and intensely opposite, that no wonder if those who are realizing the transition should be almost beside themselves. When they have passed from death into life, and find themselves sitting at the feet of Jesus, clothed, and in their right mind, they have no eye for another object, no ear for another's words; they can think of nothing else, talk of nothing else, attend to nothing else, until the new consciousness becomes somewhat habitual, and the absorbing and bewildering happiness subsides into the "sober certainty of waking bliss."

Jesus knew all this better than Martha, and excused the half-tranced spirit of Mary, when her sister would have had Him reprove her for neglect of household cares; and Martha herself was admonished, though with a faultless mixture of tenderness and solicitude. "Martha, Martha, thou art careful and troubled about many things, but one thing is needful: and Mary hath chosen that good part, which shall not be taken away from her." This good part was the knowledge of the Lord Jesus as her Saviour—it was, in fact, Jesus Himself. She was not content with His being the guest of the family; not content with the privilege of listening to His conversation with her sister and brother. She had heard Him say that He was a Shepherd, seeking lost sheep and lambs, and *she* had strayed from the fold. Mary had found no portion in the wilderness; no shelter for her fears, no promise of *the green pastures* and *the still waters* so congenial with the deep thoughtfulness of her spirit, and *there* was the Shepherd Himself, and he had bent His eye upon her, and in that eye, glistening and running over with the light of love, she saw a welcome and drew near to His feet; she felt that He was about to die for her, and ventured upon His mercy. And now her heart was burdened with love, and she cried, *What can I do for Him?* She uttered no loud professions of attachment, no avowals of the great things she *would* do if she had the power; but she began to do what she could. Her love was too genuine to allow her hands to be still. Now that her heart had found its object she would evince a carefulness, a diligence, a practical aim that should outstrip Martha herself. And what could she do for Christ? *Martha* was anxious that He should lack no comfort while He abode with them in Bethany; and she served Him with all the love, reverence, and industry of which her nature was capable. The *Magdalene, Joanna, Susanna,* and others, followed Him from place to place, ministering to Him of their substance: what could *Mary* do? Was there no room in His service for a meeker and more retired spirit than theirs? Yes, her faith instructed her; she had heard Him speak of His death; perhaps her woman's heart had gone further into this mystery than the faith of the apostles; for when Christ declared the necessity of His death to them, they replied, Be it far from thee, Lord! but when He spake of it to her, she prepared an anointing for His burial! It would be too much to say that Mary apprehended fully the meaning of the Saviour's death; but she seems to have known that that death was a part of His mission on earth, and an event vitally affecting her salvation; and she would do what in her lay to put honor upon it; she would spare from her own limited means, hoard the money which a Jewish maiden delighted to spend upon ornaments, and purchase an unguent, costly and precious, to pour upon His head ere it was bowed in death for her, and to anoint those gracious feet at which she first tasted His love.

The act was singular, the price of the ointment extravagant, she was a woman, and one peculiarly averse to display; her zeal would be called forwardness, the offering of her self-denying love would be censured as waste, her motive would be misunderstood; but faith raised Mary above every personal consideration; she was simply the handmaid of her Master; and she meant to glorify *Him;* her single eye was so clear and heavenly, that she rendered this service unconscious of herself, and, it may be, of the presence of others, until the silence and wonder of the company, before whom she did it, were broken by the complaint of Judas Iscariot. Whenever we desire to offer up anything to Jesus, there is always some Judas at hand on the side of economy and propriety to dissuade us from doing it. "Whence this waste!" cried the covetous hypocrite, "the ointment might have been sold for three hundred pence and given to the poor." Three hundred pence is £9 16s. of our money; a large gift for Mary, but she felt that even this was not enough—*Too much!* She might have said,

> Too much to Thee I cannot give,
> Too much I cannot do for Thee;
> Let all Thy love and all Thy grief
> Graven on my heart for ever be.

And they *were* graven on Mary's heart; and how her spirit must have thrilled with gratitude and triumph when her Lord silenced the rude and malignant tongue of the adversary, and vindicated the heart that had placed at His feet its costliest gift, and its entire service. "Let her alone!" cried He, as poor accused Mary was wiping His feet with her hair, "against the day of my burial hath she kept this. For the poor always ye have with you, but me ye have not always." *He* was not wont to neglect the poor who used to feed them by thousands together. He was not wont to sanction extravagance, who on every occasion commanded that the fragments should be gathered up and nothing lost. But the heart that gives itself to Jesus, leaves no fragments to be gathered; its gifts are not selected, numbered, weighed, and valued; everything goes in, and all is too little! Mark the honor with which Mary's act was crowned: "Verily I say unto you, Wheresoever this gospel shall be preached throughout the whole world, this also that she hath done shall be spoken of for a memorial of her." And the Lord has honored Mary's deed with this celebrity, not that she may be admired simply, but *imitated*.

My dear young friends, Mary's was a wise choice, for she chose the best portion. It was best because it comprehended every other. When the Lord is our portion, there is not a single want of body, mind, or heart, unprovided for; and the blessings by which these wants are supplied may come and go without touching the portion itself. The Giver is ours, ours *eternally;* the gifts are for a season, and are subject to the fluctuations of occasion and want. Riches take to themselves wings, and carry off with them distinctions, luxury, and friends; beauty enjoys its morning triumph like the flower, and dies at noon; youth frequently dies with it, and the glorious vigour of manhood follows, and man soon lieth down and riseth not. Children are the Lord's heritage. He gives them and He takes them, but Himself remains the portion, *I will never leave thee*. The secret of a Christian's steady unbroken happiness is this; he makes no blessing his portion, but Him with whom is the *power* of blessing. Choose Christ, and you choose *all* with Him, all that may be necessary in time and beyond time. This is particularly noticed in the text, "Mary hath chosen that good part, *which shall not be taken away from her;*" and so strictly and affectingly true is this, that Jesus is never so precious as when everything else is wanting;

> Though waves and storms go o'er my head,
>   Though strength, and health, and friends be gone;
> Though joys be withered all and dead,
>   Though every comfort be withdrawn;
> On this my steadfast soul relies;
> Jesus my *portion* never dies.

But Mary's was a universal choice, it was the choice of her whole being. Her judgment and conscience consented to the truth of her Saviour's words; she had sufficient taste to discriminate and admire the beauty and value of His religion, but her heart was as ready to love as her understanding to approve. She did not choose Christ as a portion she might want bye and bye, when youth had left her, and the season of pleasure and vanity had passed; when sickness would cut off ease and comfort; when age would leave her without a friend. Her heart had no rival, her prudence no reservation, her purpose no condition; thought, feeling, sympathy, passion, all consented to the choice; it was the better part for them all; and then, and there, she gave herself a whole burnt offering to the Lord. What an insult to Christ to offer Him the approval of our judgment, and reserve for other things the devotion of our heart; and yet many of you are living under the ban of this dishonor. You would be ashamed not to profess to believe and respect the Saviour: you are not ashamed to sin against the Saviour: but this divided service, this convenient compact with religion, stipulating for its respectability and for its assistance when nothing else will help you, a disposition to allow, and a repugnance to do and suffer, must end in shame. I hope you know this; I hope that your judgment is not so far reprobate as not to condemn you for it, that your conscience is not so far hardened as not to wound you for it. O confess all at His feet as Mary did! and since He once more offers Himself as your portion, accept Him this moment!

SERMON XVIII.

Gen. v. 24.

"*And Enoch walked with God: and he was not; for God took him.*"

Between the creation of man and the destruction of his race by the flood, there was a period of one thousand six hundred and fifty-five years. Yet the history of these centuries is condensed into four chapters; and the lives of the great men who flourished during the antediluvian epoch are nearly all brought within the chapter before us. Two or three verses are allotted to each; wherein it is briefly stated that they lived, begat children, and died. They were all nearly contemporary with each other: for Adam lived to see Methuselah, the grandfather of Noah. What customs and habits they followed, how they lived, what cities, and how many, they built, the Holy Spirit has not deemed it necessary to inform their descendants. Their lives were nine times as long as ours, and their physical condition was, perhaps, as much superior to ours. It is not so clear that their intellectual character corresponded with it. We read of Jabal the tent-maker and shepherd, of Jubal the musician, and of Tubal Cain the discoverer of metals; but it is doubtful whether their achievements went beyond their necessities; and almost certain that they had no literature. Their moral state, with one or two shining exceptions, was deplorable. Adam had numerous children: but it was two hundred years after the birth of Cain before a religious society was formed. The first church was planted in the family of Seth, when he and his son Enos *began to call upon the name of the Lord.* The brightest star of the few lights that shone out from the antediluvian gloom, was Enoch, the son of Jared, and the seventh from Adam. From a brief record preserved in the Bible, it would appear that Enoch's spiritual life began when he was sixty-five years old: that is, after the birth of his son Methuselah: that the testimony he then received, that he pleased God, advanced him to so close a fellowship with the Deity, that after preaching against the rebellion and depravity of those corrupt times for three hundred years, he was permitted to escape the pang of man's last hour, passing up to glory in the light of life, instead of from the darkness of the tomb.

Enoch was probably a teacher and prophet by profession. St. Jude has given us an extract from his predictions. "And Enoch also," writes this Apostle, "the seventh from Adam, prophesied of these, saying, Behold, the Lord cometh with ten thousand of his saints, to execute judgment upon all, and to convince all that are ungodly among them of all their ungodly deeds which they have ungodly committed, and of all their hard speeches which ungodly sinners have spoken against him." It has been supposed that this quotation was taken from the *Book of Enoch*, an apocryphal work. There is a frequent reference to this book in the pages of the old fathers; but for several centuries the Enoch manuscript was missing; and it was not until James Bruce, the traveller, picked up this curious relic in Abyssinia, that criticism was able to verify the extracts found in the writings of the early church, and to pronounce upon the authenticity of the book. Bruce found it in an Æthiopic version, and incorporated by the Abyssinians with their books of the Old Testament. Many of its descriptions resemble so closely portions of the Apocalypse, that it is difficult to believe it was not written after that book, and therefore subsequently to Jude's epistle. Be this as it may, whether

Jude extracted his passage from the work in question, or found it among the traditions of the Jewish fathers, there can be no reasonable doubt that the quotation is genuine: and, as casting one or two rays of historic light upon a period beyond the sphere of history, it is a fragment unspeakably precious. We may learn from it that in antediluvian times God raised up a ministry of holy men to preach His judgments, predict His coming, and preserve His worship. Enoch and Noah were among these ancient preachers, by whose faithful labours the Spirit of God strove with the old world. That age was darker than any that has followed it: yet even then there lived men whom the Holy Ghost has thought fit to set forth as examples to the church in all ages.

We have said that Adam was still living when Enoch flourished: and the younger saint might have been often seen visiting the tent of the illustrious father of man, to hear the story of Adam's creation and fall. We can imagine old Adam striving to recall for young Enoch's sake the felicities of the first Eden; describing to the listener the sublime elevation of his soul before he stooped to transgression, his converse with God and angels, his happy freedom from sin and dread, the health and beauty of his person, and the innumerable delights of his position. But especially would the first Adam speak to his disciple of a *second Adam*, and of the promise regarding the seed of the woman bruising the serpent's head. Enoch, however, went to a higher source than Adam to learn of Christ. He retired from men to increase the illumination he had received from the conversation of others. A glimmering of the truth drew him to the fountain of light, and there he poured out his heart, beseeching that God would reveal to him the hope of the world more distinctly, and vouchsafe the salvation of a holy faith in the Messiah; and God seems to have taken Enoch into very close communion. The path of the patriarch became *like the shining light*, shining with clearer and further-reaching beams, until he saw before him not only his own journey to heaven, but the high road upon which the nations of distant ages would press into the kingdom of God. Such, even in that dark time, was the progress of a saint of the Lord.

The figure employed to illustrate Enoch's piety is very expressive: he *walked with God*. The idea suggested by it is companionship. Two walk together because they are agreed. To produce fellowship of this kind, there must be a unity of purpose and of taste, a correspondence of circumstances, and a harmony of will. We can admire a man's character without walking with him: we can converse with him, transact business with him, receive favours from him, or confer favours upon him, without walking with him: we can dwell with him in the same house, meet him at the same table, and exchange with him the courtesies of daily life, without walking with him. There is a general benevolence or humanity that engenders what is called politeness, that is, kindness seasonably offered: and even where the temper is extinct, the gracious form is preserved; nothing is commonly more unreal, yet nothing is more necessary, than politeness. But the man with whom I walk is my friend. I have proved his character, and find it sound: I have tasted his conversation, and not only approve his opinions but imbibe his spirit. I have watched the issues of his heart and found their counterpart in my own bosom. He may be separated from me, I still walk with him: his profession may be opposite to mine, I still walk with him: his attainments and rank may look down upon mine, I still walk with him. But the foundation of this friendship is a common humanity. I doubt whether a man and an angel could commune with so entire a union. Then how are we to conceive of a man walking with God? What have they in common, the Creator and the creature? What mutual ground in the two natures in which to plant *friendship?* God is the Ancient of days; man fleeth like the shadow of a day. God is the builder of the universe; man, an insect that flits within the building. God embraces all knowledge, and is the fountain of wisdom; man knows nothing, not even himself. God is righteous and of immaculate purity; man is a fallen being, selfish and corrupt in constitution, base and mischievous in practice, erring and reprobate in judgment. God is good, lovely in goodness, tender in sympathy, and universally kind; man is a little, narrow, hard, selfish soul; proud as the heavens, small and vile as the dust; rebelling against his God, hating his brother, and living for himself. Upon what analogy of nature or of disposition, can there be intimacy between God and man? I can imagine the Creator demanding homage from man, giving him laws, appointing the bounds of his habitation, and permitting him to live upon His bounty : I can imagine God making known His will to man, and placing him under a government adapted to his nature: I can imagine God even speaking to man through the medium of an angel or an element: but how can we understand the Most High taking a man's soul and locking it in His own in the embraces of friendship; walking with him in the retired and confiding converse of an intimate relationship?

My brethren, there is more than we conceive in the meaning of that verse, "And God said, let us make man in our image, after our likeness. So God created man in his own image, in the image of God created he him." Whatever be the meaning of *likeness* and *image*, they must imply, I think, natural affinity. They cannot be limited to the dominion which was given to man over inferior creatures; nor do they express simply the spirituality and immortality of man's nature. We believe there are family features between God and man, which prove that one is the father and the other is the child. It would seem that the mind and heart of man formed originally an epitome of God Himself; that the manifestations of the intellect and the temper resembled those of the Deity; that the language of the heart was the same, and that the aims of the understanding and the bias of the will followed the purposes of God. Man, it appears to us, was created altogether for a family union with His Maker: hence so much has been done to restore him. God has pursued His wandering offspring with a father's yearnings. When angels fell, they were consigned to destruction: when man sinned, it was the rebellion of a son, not the treason of a subject. The father condemned and punished, but He could not destroy. He loved His own image; and the human spirit, although soiled and disfigured, had attractions for *Him;* and a remembrance of its former loveliness stirred the parent's affection, raised its tone to inconceivable ardour and power, and put it upon the labour of recovering the fallen child. See this relationship further illustrated in the method of our salvation. God became *man.* He made Himself man; and if the distance between the two natures is infinite in degree, it is not so in kind. How naturally do they blend in Christ! How easily are the powers of the Deity developed through human senses and faculties; as if that the latter had been cast in the mould of the former. We observe nothing violent, nothing ungraceful, no inequalities in the character of Christ. The God and the man are so intimately mingled that the line which separates them is often invisible. They have the unity of one existence. We must also remark, that after Christ had redeemed us by His death, He arose from the dead with a glorified body, and ascended to His Father and to our Father a perfect man, the representative of a restored race. God wears our nature still, and is the "order" and pattern after which His "brethren" will be formed. This, we think, is the secret of God's permitting man to walk with Him. There is a divinity in man's nature not totally effaced by sin: some features of the Godhead are yet expressed in humanity, and the affection of the heavenly Parent for His degenerate and fallen family has moved Him to restore to *glory, honor, and immortality*, all who desire to return and be reconciled to Him. Enoch walked with God because he yielded to the Spirit that drew him to God; drew him until he passed from the tabernacle of nature to the spiritual court of the true worshipper. The nearer he approached God, the more distinctly conscious was he of a *home feeling*. His powers had become deranged in other climes; but this atmosphere of heaven was native air, and the strayed child recovered his own strength and nobleness under the Father's roof.

My brethren, what is the meaning of walking with God in these times? In Enoch's days it consisted of retiring from the world and climbing sublime altitudes of devotion.

But what is the altitude of modern piety? Alas, it may hardly be called walking after God, much less *with Him!* Many of us do not inquire for Him, and the world hateth Him. But you, brethren, have professed to come out from the world; you permit yourselves to be called the disciples of a pure and world-denouncing faith; you have enrolled yourselves for a pilgrimage to the better land; you have been registered as the children of Enoch, of Noah, of Abraham; the successors of John and Paul; the fellow-heirs and brethren of Christ. But how can you link your names with this genealogy if you do not walk with God? The man who consorts with a loftier spirit than his own, grows like his companion. In such society his faculties are kept at their full tension. The powerful intellect of the superior commands his imitation; he adopts his sentiments, insensibly copies his diction and address, and catches inspiration from his spirit. Do you bear the marks of daily communion with God?

Let us now consider the means by which our walk with God may resemble in its fellowship and progress that of the very eminent patriarch before us. Enoch's piety is not inimitable. We must take care lest we regard the saints of the Bible rather as objects of reverence than as patterns of life. We must *follow* those who through faith and patience inherit the promises. It was not by an exclusive favour that Enoch gained so rare an intimacy with the Father of spirits. There was no apartment in the heavenly mansions erected solely for Enoch. As a member of the general assembly and church of the firstborn, he claimed no brighter revelations and aspired to no higher privileges than those that were offered for the attainment of his brethren. The testimony of the Epistle to the Hebrews sets this question at rest :—" By *faith* Enoch was translated that he should not see death." Again, " Before his translation he had this testimony, that he pleased God." It was *faith* that drew God to him, and brought upon his heart the rays of the divine complacency, for the writer affirms in the next verse that, " without faith it is impossible to please God :" but through faith we may open with him the most secret and familiar converse, if we " diligently seek him." The word here rendered, *diligently seek*, means to search out, to seek that which has been lost until it be found; implying diligent inquiry and painful efforts. Now, if God honored Enoch by unusual distinctions, Enoch first glorified God by following hard after him. Enoch believed that the riches of the divine glory would reward this noble toil; and he was not disappointed. God is *the rewarder of them that diligently seek Him.*

It is true that in some sense we may find God without a painful search: for whether we inquire after Him or not, He makes Himself known to us. Everything around us is full of God. No thoughtful mind can resist a certain indescribable influence in nature by which God brings His existence home to the heart. In this sense philosophers have found God, and poets have sung of Him. He has been manifest to them who asked not after Him: but God has not rewarded them with His friendship. There are others who inquire at a diviner oracle than science, and profess a holier religion than poetry, yet cannot be said to walk with God. They have casually looked about for Him, and having learned that no man cometh to the Father but by the Son, they have sought Him through Christ: they have obtained a glimpse of the divine glory, but ask for no further revelation. God never *walks* with these. They have not diligently sought Him, or rather, they have not ardently continued their search. God is not found at once. No being may be said to find Him absolutely; to possess Him wholly. The most favoured worshipper has only discovered a *portion* of God. He is like a mine; the treasures of His being are gathered by the diligent, and they who toil the hardest bring away the most. They who follow him through those passages of His wisdom, power, and mercy that have been opened to the inquirer, and who at every revelation thirst for more secret and sublime disclosures, find their way at last to the hand and heart of the Deity. Let us not imagine that our knowledge of God has reached its climax when faith in Christ has reconciled us to Him. Intercourse is but then begun; the field of a glorious fellowship is then thrown open; and if the soul set forth, nobly resolved to improve the privileges earned for it by the sufferings and death of Jesus, there will be efforts more strenuous, and conflicts more painful, and changes more striking after its reconciliation with God than there were before it. How mean the thought that we know enough of God when we have learned that He is not our enemy! If anything can move the contempt of an angel, it is a man who having tasted that the Lord is gracious, cries "Enough!" To be brought to the foot of the mountain of holiness and not dare to venture up! Venture, did we say—let us not say venture, for we are not come unto the mount that burned with fire, nor unto blackness, and darkness, and tempest, and the sound of a trumpet, and the voice of words; for then might a Moses exclaim, *I exceedingly fear and quake.* "But we are come unto Mount Zion, to the city of the living God;" and yet we are too indolent to go up and enter in! We are come to "an innumerable company of angels," who beckon us to climb higher, and stretch out a thousand hands to minister to us and help us up; and yet we ignobly stand at the bottom of the mount. We are come to "the church of the first-born, which are written in heaven;" we have seen them go up before us; we have seen Enoch under the force of his sublime aspirations climb to the summit of holy Zion, and enter the cloud of the Divine Majesty; we have seen Noah climb after him; and Abraham and the Patriarchs, Moses and the Prophets, Paul and the Apostles, Stephen and the Martyrs, we have seen the spirits of the just go up, and *their feet stand within thy gates, O Jerusalem!* and yet this imposing array of witnesses, stretching over the vast Bible history, has not excited within us a heavenly ambition to emulate their career, a spark of holy rivalry! We are come "to Jesus the mediator of the new covenant, and to the blood of sprinkling," and yet we do not ask what that covenant has made over to us, and what that blood can do for us. That covenant confers the right of an abundant entrance into God, and yet we are satisfied if it saves us from hell; that covenant is our passport to the inner chamber of the Divine presence, the chamber of visions and revelations, where the most undisguised utterances are heard, and where the soul recovers the image of her Maker; and yet with the Testament of our dying Lord in our hand, bequeathing to us these exalted honors, we do not press on to make them our own! And the blood of sprinkling we are prone to think has done all that is needful when it justifies us; when it turns back from us the judgments of the law. We seem to forget that it cleanses from all sin, and thus removes the grand objection to our walking with God.

O brethren, are we come to these examples and helps, by the aid of which we may attain the heights of Zion, and enter into that sacred fellowship with God with which Enoch was honored, and do we stand at a distance from our Creator? Let us mourn and weep over this unnatural conduct; let each one arise and go to his Father, and say, "I have sinned against heaven and in thy sight:" let us with sincere humility and with the emotions and resolves of penitence fall at His feet, confess our almost unpardonable disobedience, and plead for the intercession of our *Elder Brother, that we may obtain mercy, and grace to help* us for a new career in the Christian life!

SERMON XIX.

GEN. v. 24.

"*And Enoch walked with God: and he was not; for God took him.*"

IF a passion for gold can swallow up other interests, and make men leave their homes, sacrifice their comforts, and even peril their lives, shall a passion for God be less potent? Shall this not be able to master other desires, and subordinate other pursuits, and inspire an equal spirit of self-denial? Let us, dear brethren, strive to approach unto God; it will cost an effort, but the object will recompense the toil. We are in pursuit of God, and He meets our discouragements with the promise, "They that seek me shall find me." It is not an enterprise of doubtful issue; for our exertions receive a constant stimulus from certain earnests of success which the Lord lays in the seeker's path. We are not allowed to grope after God in utter darkness. He affords cheering intimations that He is not far from us. He draws us after Him, increases the light on our path, and ordains that we *shall walk and not faint.* We need not borrow the index of human science; nor puzzle and tire ourselves with metaphysical questions. Philosophy cannot "show us the Father." The Lord Jesus leads us to God, and whither He goes, we know; and the way we know. He that hath seen Him, hath seen the Father. We cannot, in our sinful state, dwell with definite ideas on the purely spiritual existence of God; but the fulness of the Godhead, dwelling bodily in the man Christ Jesus, is represented in a form upon which we can look,—a person; and, O the marvellous ways of God! in a person of our own nature. The overwhelming glory of the Deity is softened through the beautiful and perfect humanity of Christ. God cannot commune with us apart from His Son. The clearest revelation which he has made of himself, is called, *the truth as it is in Jesus.* Prayer, which is the main help of the soul's walking with God, is only accepted through Jesus; and when Paul, in a grand petition, asks that the riches of the divine glory may be granted to the Ephesians, he adds this most needful supplication, "That Christ may dwell in your hearts by faith;" and when his prayer rises to an almost perilous sublimity; when his large apostolic soul, transported with the freedom and immensity of grace, prays that they may be filled with all the fullness of God, he makes this the result of knowing *the love of Christ, which passeth knowledge*. And of the spirits that from the margin of death have plunged into this fullness, of those who dwell with God in the sinless and immortal regions of heaven, we read that *there* they worship and meditate and live through Jesus. The Lamb who saved them on earth, is now *in the midst of the throne*, feeding them, and leading them *unto living fountains of water*. Let me exhort you to cultivate a deeper acquaintance with the Saviour. You have seen His arm and felt its power; tell Him, you want a larger place in His heart; you want to read His life, and ever to place it before you as the pattern of your own; tell Him you want your spirit to take root in the deep things of God, especially in that deepest of all, His own love. If in earnest and firm resolve you make the Lord Jesus your portion, and Him only, and Him always, He will with sympathetic affection lead you into the more secret repositories of grace, give you more of the knowledge and secure for you more of the friendship of His Father and your Father, than you can either ask or think. "Eye hath not seen, nor ear heard, neither have entered into the heart of man, the things which God hath prepared for them that love Him."

Let us now follow Enoch to the crown of his piety. *God took him.* It is scarcely necessary to prove that neither these words, nor that passage in the Hebrews founded upon them, can be fairly interpreted to mean anything else than a miraculous translation to heaven. The language that registers the departure of every patriarch in this chapter, except Enoch, is simply, *he died.* We may hence conclude that when Moses writes concerning Enoch that *God took him*, he does not vary the description of an ordinary death, but records a singular and extraordinary fact, that men found not Enoch, because God had translated him. Moreover, the word used in the text to signify Enoch's departure, is found no where else in the Old Testament to mean *death;* but it is employed in the Book of Kings to describe Elijah's removal—" And it came to pass, when the Lord would *take up* Elijah."

The writer of the Epistle to the Hebrews ought to have precluded all criticism on this subject. But a miracle like the translation of Enoch involves a too credulous acceptance of the supernatural; it is also a needless demand upon our faith, when a slight modification of the text will reduce the wonder to a very natural event. It has therefore been suggested that the difficulty in the passage of the Epistle be got rid of in this manner—" By faith Enoch was translated that he should die suddenly by lightning, for before his translation he had this testimony that he pleased God."(!) But surely a license like this, makes criticism a ploughshare instead of a pruning-knife; and the fairest gardens of literature would soon be a wilderness, if this rude, this most unscholarly treatment of an ancient author were permitted in the elucidation of classical learning. In the instance before us, our English version is a faithful copy of the original text: and giving the writer credit for meaning what he said, and not supposing that he accommodated his description to any tradition existing among the Jews, the statement may be relied on, that Enoch, like Elijah, was taken up to heaven without dying.

The scriptures say nothing of the manner of this translation; nor indeed of the reason of it. The latter may be conjectured. It is not improbable that it had reference to the age in which Enoch lived. We have already, in a former discourse, referred to the depravity of the antedeluvian world. Men lived in that age for eight centuries. When the opening of a grave was so unusual an occurrence, heaven or another state might soon be forgotten. Even in our day, when life is brief and mortality incessant, it is hard to awaken a serious thought on eternity. And in Enoch's times it might have been necessary by some wonder or prodigy to arouse men from the stupidity and ignorance of centuries: and the sudden vanishing of Enoch in the midst of his years by a miraculous translation was adapted to produce this effect. The news of the patriarch's ascension must have electrified the fathers of the ancient world. They were the immediate descendants of Adam, but had never imagined the possibility of this miracle. Every one of the departed had bowed to the decree, "Dust thou art, and unto dust shalt thou return." The old men had mournfully followed their father Adam to the grave; Eve was laid beside him; and they had no other notion of their end but that since the father and mother of the race had *gathered up their feet*, it was appointed unto them all once to die. But the translation of Enoch convinced them that there was something in man above the law of mortality. Enoch was born amongst them; they had seen his infancy, youth, and manhood; he was subject to the same wants and carried the same infirmities as they; and yet he had escaped *death*, the uniform issue of want and weakness. Thoughts like these would stir up among them a questioning as to the reason of Enoch's deliverance from the grave, and they would recur to his life. *There was the secret of his miraculous exit.* They would remember something in his life that disdained submission to death. They would remember his sermons; for Enoch like Noah was *a preacher of righteousness;* they would recall his declamations against their wickedness; his testimony of the Messiah, and of the day in which God would judge the world. They had, perhaps, regarded him as a visionary, a man of solitary walks and musings; perhaps they had sported with his piety as the dream of an enthusiast; and even persecuted the messenger of God when he followed them to the haunts of their unlawful pleasures, and boldly witnessed against their sins. But now they saw the end of that holy and benevolent life; they saw the poor visionary conveyed away beyond the stars! Here was the power of goodness: Enoch was borne away above the tombs of his fathers, proving that a higher world, a nobler existence, awaited the seeker of God. The mantle of Enoch's testimony fell; and one would think it should not have fallen in vain. Those among his brethren who called upon the name of the Lord began to revive the expectation of the Messiah. In Enoch's own family this hope was so strong that Lamech, his grandson, called his eldest child *Noah*, under an impatient supposition that he was the promised deliverer,—" This child," said his father, " shall comfort us concerning our work and the toil of our hands, because of the ground which the Lord hath cursed."

We have dwelt upon the manner and reason of Enoch's translation: it remains for us to consider the event itself as the consummation of a holy life. " Enoch walked with God; and he was not; for God took him." Here is the probationary character of piety. Enoch walked with God first, and then God took him; removed him from earth; from the shifting tent of pilgrimage to the abodes of immortality. With those blemishes of frailty which no degree of intelligence can efface, with laws of physical nature limiting his intellectual faculties, it was 'impossible for Enoch to walk with God in perfect intimacy. There was an immense reserve both of emotion and understanding that could never get into action on earth. He loved God: but how imperfectly awakened even this passion, cultivated though it was to the highest pitch of sacredness and friendship, compared with what it would be in the heavenly state. When the soul of the patriarch had passed through the rude gradations of an immortal life; when by instruction, regeneration, affliction, labour, and many severe encounters and exercises of faith, courage, and endurance, Enoch had been prepared for the glorious life of heaven, God set him free from those laws that hold us to the dust, exalted his vision above the horizon of a terrestrial sphere, unbound the wings of his spirit, and bade it fly homeward. Enoch had often gone thither by faith, had often gazed through the telescope of hope upon those fair landscapes which stretch away from the other side of a good man's grave; but now faith was cast off like a mantle, hope was undistinguishable in the realization of its dreams, and love, that crowning and immortal grace, found itself rolling to God, its fountain and ocean, like a river freed from its embankments. The ascending prophet rising through the grosser medium of sense, gained the element of pure spirit, and resumed his study of God in happy freedom from the vile restrictions of mortality. Before his translation, he pleased God as an infant pleases its father. Its imperfect imitations of speech, its little struggles to grasp an idea, its prattlings and questions charm the tender and watchful parent, because they indicate the shape of the future man. We can imagine no gratification more exquisite than a father's joy, as he observes the unfoldings of that beautiful flower, a child's mind; unless indeed it be the chastened triumph with which he afterwards points to the happy results of his training in the boy now grown to manhood; capable of discourse and counsel; qualified to hold up his head among his father's friends, and to augment the importance of his father's house; then the cup of parental bliss overflows. Now God rejoices over His children in this manner, but in a far higher degree. Enoch was a child on earth; he walked with God, but his steps were feeble, his progress slow; he called upon the name of his Father, but the call was a lisp, the broken accents of infancy. He learned from the volume of God's works, and conned over the lessons of His grace; but his highest efforts were little more than a spelling out the simplest passages of providence and mercy; but there was *growth*. Enoch's heart went before his intellect. The child loved his Father before he understood Him; and love is that feature in the divine image in which God most delights. An early affection has more charm for Him, than a precocious intelligence. The first and great commandment is, Thou shalt *love*, not, Thou shalt *know*. The builder and master of the human mind has made it to act with the greatest freedom and success when it is moved by love. If this be the dominant feeling it hallows every other passion; and it also imparts to the reason a clearness, to the understanding a strength, to the fancy a warmth, and to the will a gentleness and humility, which ensure the very highest results in intellectual inquiry. God does not seem to have intended any great general triumphs for the intellect on earth; he holds this in abeyance and calls out the emotive faculties. The reason of man will perhaps do wonders in heaven; but the love of God must first do wonders on earth. The expansion of the understanding is reserved for that world where sin cannot corrupt and failure and sorrow cannot depress it. Hence God contemns human wisdom, as such; but honors every symptom of holy affection; and the humble soul who knows little and loves much, is a more choice intelligence than the man of science, although before men the latter be a prodigy of intellectual power.

It is delightful to reflect upon the sudden enlargement of a mind like Enoch's transported to heaven in the twinkling of an eye! What a glorious birth there must have been of power to think, and of capacity to love! What an instantaneous accession of ideas! When Enoch entered heaven, no Saviour had gone down to redeem the world; the glorious company of the apostles had not been formed, the noble martyrs had not bled for the Cross, and the church of the first-born numbered but three or four souls, Abel, Enoch, Adam, and a few others. But these were enough to begin the new song, *Unto Him that loved us, &c.* Although the sacrifice was not offered, it was made in purpose, and they felt they were blood-bought souls. We may imagine the angels gathering about this little band, and asking each other the meaning of the anthem in which they were unable to join; we can suppose that these blessed first-fruits would make the host of heaven yearn for the harvest-time, when that dark and distant earth would return, not her twos and threes, but her millions to augment the population of the skies, and crown the work of the Son of God. Enoch could doubtless descry the line of ages and events through which the gospel scheme would run,—its superficial trials and changes, its resistless progress, its infallible success and final triumph. What Enoch foresaw in vision we have seen in accomplishment. Heaven will be very different now from what Enoch found it. To be translated now, when the redeeming work is finished! When He that went forth, *travelling in the greatness of His strength*, has returned from Edom and from Bozrah, with His garments dyed in the blood of His enemies, and His brows graced with the many crowns of His achievements. Enoch found heaven a field of expectation; we shall find it a scene of triumph; Enoch conversed with Christ on the decease He should accomplish; we shall congratulate Him on what He has accomplished. Enoch found but a few companions to enter with him into the immediate visions of the Divine glory; we shall greet numbers without number, of every kindred, with Jesus at their head; a sight that Enoch saw not for ages after his translation. Heaven was worth living for in Enoch's time; it is worth dying for now! We cling to life as if death were our greatest affliction; we battle with disease as if it would sever us from happiness for ever; we mourn for them that are gone as if the saddest fate had overtaken them: but if *we* know it not, *they* know it, that heaven is worth dying for. O, brethren, live for heaven, and think it not a hard fate that, like Enoch, we cannot escape thither without passing through the valley of death! It is no disgrace to die: the humiliation of the grave is no more: Christ has wiped off its reproach. The stroke from which we shrink, He felt; and O, how keenly, how ignominiously! But from that hour, it was written, *Blessed are the dead which die in the Lord.* Sorrow for the happy dead has no ground or reason apart from ourselves. We ought to call them the *happy living.* They may well mourn for us, if there be weeping in heaven. *We* are buried, and not *they.* We lie in tombs of ignorance and sin, and they walk over the earth that covers us. The restraint, the corruption, the insensibility, is ours: theirs the liberty, the purity, the vigor, and the happiness of life. We speak of them as memories of yesterday, of last year, of last century: *we* are memories and not *they :* they are recollecting *us,* not we them. We are in the past, and they look back upon us over centuries of advancement. To them secrets are unveiled and events known which this plodding earth will not discover or understand for ages. The onward thinkers of mankind and the most enlightened and effective agents in all the important movements of the human race are in heaven, and working with us from there! *The fathers, where are they?* In understanding and experience more worthy of their fatherhood than when they instructed us on earth. *The prophets, do they live for ever?* Live! Yes, in the glorious fruition of their predictions. *Man giveth up the ghost, and where is he?* In his own rightful immortality, thinking without weariness or failure, and labouring with unfettered powers and with infinite results. We can thus fill up nearly all the blanks of the Old Testament by the revelations of the New. By the torch of the New Testament we can read the problem of a grave: listen to its grand rendering, *Sown in corruption; raised in incorruption: sown in dishonor; raised in glory: sown in weakness; raised in power: sown a natural body raised a spiritual body.*

SERMON XX.

ISAIAH lxi. 3.

"*Beauty for ashes.*"

THIS is the mission of Christianity: it finds ashes; it gives beauty. Man resembles a palace in ruins; the touching and impressive remains of what was once noble and splendid. We gaze upon the human race with feelings not unlike the melancholy awakened in some ancient and dilapidated mansion. Here rose the towers, proud heralds of majesty; that fragment of a column marks what was once the royal entrance; and the enclosure in which we stand, roofless and matted with wild grass, was a hall of state; and the passages we are threading, dark and dank, noisome and obscene, where birds of darkness flit and scream, once led to the sumptuous apartments of beauty and chivalry : we climb a piece of old ivied wall and look about us : we observe that the ruin imparts a gloom to all the landscape : nature sympathizes and suffers with it : everything upon which its shadows fall looks old and venerable for its sake.

Such a grand old ruin is the human race: it was built in paradise, with attributes rising like towers to the skies; the habitation of God, the resort of angels, the glory of earth, which had no beauty of herself, but that which was reflected upon her from him who was created in the image of God. But sin entered humanity, and death by sin; and, agreeably to that retributive law, *when Thou with rebukes dost correct man for iniquity, Thou makest his beauty to consume away like a moth*, the structure became ashes. We cannot take our stand outside this ruin, and look at it from positions of contrast, to observe its gigantic outline standing clear against the light of heaven, because we ourselves are the ruin. We never could have discovered it, or been made conscious of it, but by the revelation of God. The divine word instructs us, and the Holy Spirit makes us feel, that we are little more than a fragment of what we once were. Our thoughts on almost any subject are small, indistinct, and without authority: the will that should rule us is our slave; the passions that should obey us are our masters; the tastes of a God-like intelligent being are reversed. We gravitate towards earth and hell; with the propensities of a worm, we bore our way through clods of grossness, and make ourselves the bed of a worm: morally, as well as materially, we may " say to corruption, Thou art my father, and to the worm, Thou art my mother and my sister." It is the law of spirit to go upwards; but unless the breath of a new life quicken him, man, materialized and brutalized by sin, is ever sinking, ever falling, through stages of sin, ignorance, and misery, further and further from God, until His nature merges in the Satanic, and God Himself cannot restore him.

As an illustration of these statements, I need not fetch a cannibal from Fiji; I need not take you from this city. Can there be a more impressive picture of an intellect in ashes than a man bowing his knee to a bit of wood, or offering up the reverence of his judgment and his trust to a beast? And when you behold all this country of India, with its many millions of souls; when you examine the foundation upon which they build their hope for eternity; when you consider the ridiculous folly of their gravest speculations; when you reflect that, what they call their religion is a system of gigantic vices, giving scope and stimulus to that very nature which religion was intended to destroy; when you observe, though without surprise, that the spirit of the people answers to these appalling superstitions, in the almost helpless violation of all morality, in the habitual prostitution of truth, purity, and honesty, in a universal incapacity for generous and manly deeds; when above all you find them a learned people, and that these abominations are sanctioned by their moralists, statesmen, and poets; when wickedness is inculcated in *schools;* is anything wanted to complete a most perfect example of man in ashes, man without form, either as an individual mind, or as a community of minds? And is it not true that his mournful ruin shades and saddens everything else? The moral landscape seems to blight the physical. In spite of the gorgeous cloud-land of these tropical skies, in spite of the florid vegetation of an Indian soil, its massive trees, its biannual harvests, its abundant fruits; no thoughtful man can walk through the country without being sickened by the poverty, the degradation, the profound stupidity, the social miseries, and the pitiful fanaticism of the people. Everything wears a heathenish aspect, except the blessed heavens, whose stars, like true evangelists, are ever preaching against those who substitute an image for *Him whom the heavens cannot contain.*

But you will find illustrations of man in ashes even in polished cities, where government, education, and wealth concur to lessen misery, to diffuse knowledge, to multiply arts of refinement, to impress order, and to teach morality. It is true that men as a general rule are richer, wiser, happier, in England than in India; but it is no less true that in both countries human nature is a ruin; it certainly has not been rebuilt in England. There is not the same appearance of dilapidation; but because a few repairs have been effected in one corner, and an apartment here and there reclaimed, we must not deceive ourselves with the notion that the edifice of humanity has been *restored*. Civilization may *cover* ashes with beauty, but it cannot give beauty *for* ashes. You may find ashes beneath the covering of man's best estate. The most improved nature, the most fortunate circumstances, will not secure us against failure, sorrow, and death. Man's happiness, such as it is, can only be counted by moments; man's best established reliances most commonly fail him, and in the hour of his greatest confidence; man's intellect, even when most continuously and successfully exerted, performs but half its task. Its efforts consist mainly of great attempts, indicating what it might have done. The works which men leave behind them in literature, mechanics, government, and arts, are little else than splendid fragments. *What might not such a man have done had he lived*, is the common epitaph of genius.

But let us narrow our observation to self; let every one of us find, as he may easily do, an example of ruin in his own nature. Have we a sound part in us? Two words will describe me thoroughly and exhaustively, *sin and ashes*. "O Israel, thou hast destroyed thyself, but in me is thy help." I feel that I am a ruin, a fragment. I can conceive what I might have been, what I may yet be; but *what I am*, except so far as the grace of God has changed me, let my frail body testify—the seat of a thousand ailments now, a little heap of dust by and by; *what I am*, let my deceitful heart reply, with not a healthy spot in it, evading by its subtlety the most careful scrutiny, and yet in its turn the veriest dupe of its own deceit; *what I am*, let my own sins bear witness. The plain path to God and heaven was shown me, I knew it to be the way of right and salvation, and heavenly motives were given to induce me to walk therein; the Spirit strove, the word instructed, example warned; but I took my own course; knew it was destruction, but still took it, and but for the restraining grace of God, I should have been in hell. *What I am*, let the law of God which I have transgressed, and the providence of God which I have tempted, and the love of God which I have despised, let these answer that, from the sole of the foot, even unto the crown of the head, I am morally, intellectually, and physically, a ruin. The depth and extent of this ruin, let the suffering Jesus reveal; He can tell who, to give me beauty, became ashes!

Now by what process does beauty spring from ashes? You have heard of that fabulous Egyptian bird, the phœnix. The ancients describe it as single, the only one of its kind; in shape like an eagle, but of more beautiful plumage. They imagined that it lived five hundred years in the wilderness, and then built a pile of aromatic wood; and setting this on fire with the wafting of its wings, consumed itself to ashes: that from the ashes arose a worm, which in time became *beauty for ashes*, another phœnix! We have no account of the origin of this fiction, but it is an exquisite type of the process by which life and organization are renewed. Ashes imply suffering and death; these lie at the foundation of beauty. *That which thou sowest is not quickened except it die, but if it die, it bringeth forth much fruit.*

We have become guilty in the sight of God; the sentence and the curse of death rest upon us; the way back to life is through ashes. Under the law, no sinner could see the beauty of the Lord, or inquire in His temple, except through *the ashes of an heifer*, or of some other animal, *sprinkling the unclean*. The consuming fire was ever kept burning upon the Jewish altar: animal life was continually suffering, animal organization was incessantly passing into ashes, and from these, as the accepted types of the last great Offering, sprang "the beauty of the Lord," shining upon the sinner's heart, conveying pardon and salvation, changing the sinner into its own image from glory to glory; and all at the price of ashes. And here we must distinguish between the positive ruin, described in the first part of this address as the personal result of man's sin and the fact of man's condition, and the vicarious sufferings and death of our Lord Jesus. We must consider Him as a member of the human family; not only suffering and dying with them, but by reason of His divine nature dying *for* them. We were consuming in the fires of sin, and should have perished in our ashes, but He threw Himself upon the pile and it became an altar of atonement: He converted the smoke of torment into the sweet incense of an oblation, and the ashes of the sacrifice became the seeds of a new race and a new earth. Beauty came forth in the person of Jesus, the first glorious fruit of suffering. In Him we see the perfection of man restored, the ruined intellect once more assuming the image of God, surpassing in *the second Adam* the intelligence of the first: we see the heart once more all glorious within, the body once more the perfection of immortal beauty; so that although " by man came death, by man came also the resurrection of the dead:" the resurrection of the spirit and the resurrection of the body. *Risen with Christ* from guilt, from misery, from ashes, there is perfect deliverance from every possible evil, through a Saviour's work and name, and the restoration of universal beauty.

From the time of Christ's ascension to glory there has been working upon the earth a resurrection power. Like the breath of the four winds that swept over the charnel-valley of the prophet, it is immediately connected with prophesying, with preaching to men the facts of Christ's work and death, and publishing the love of God who " spared not His own Son but freely delivered Him up for us all;" and this gospel is found to be a savour of life to dying souls; a proclamation and a power of liberty to those who are held fast by reigning sins; and a law of love, of civilization, and of social order to men whom ignorance and inheerent vice had driven asunder from each other; and a renovating spirit, making all things new, raising in power whatever has been sown in weakness, giving spirituality to that which is material, and changing dishonor into glory. And although it is true that the world still lieth in wickedness and spiritual death, there is a great multitude which no man can number gathered into an invisible society, composing a few apartments of the "spiritual house," which Christ the architect is raising upon the ruins of the fall. We say an invisible society, for the world cannot discern the unity of these stones, or the plan of the building as it rises from them. Yet even those who have no eye for the perception and enjoyment of heavenly forms, cannot fail to see that Christianity, whether it; spring from heaven or men, is the mightiest agency on earth. It is ever at work in the ashes of our waste places. Set it down anywhere, and wait awhile: the curse of ignorance flies before it, men know themselves, they learn the nature and the laws of their Maker; man worships his God, and embraces his fellow; his understanding is ennobled by heavenly ideas and strengthened by positive knowledge; his love, his hope, his trust, no longer the dupes of error and the slaves of lust, but raised from the mire and the clay, get wings for heaven and rest in God; the foundation of society is changed, and all its activities are directed to the elevation of the race. The transforming power of the gospel was never so rapid in its action, and its triumphs were never so conspicuous as in these days: and no antagonism shall let it, until its work is done. What is that voice that is everywhere crying out for redress, that impatience of things as they are, that now urges forward nations who for ages had never conceived such an idea as change? What mean those great political events that are clearing the Lord's path to the peoples of the earth,—breaking up caste in India, despotism in Naples, exclusiveness in China, and popery in Rome? Are not these the signs of the Lord's approach, the preliminary changes that lie between ashes and beauty?

Hitherto we have considered the text as a remarkable enunciation of the character and scope of the gospel mission, and we have made this the chief topic of our address, but we must not omit the local object of the passage. The words were spoken by Christ, and in this connexion, "The Spirit of the Lord God is upon me; because the Lord hath anointed me to preach good tidings to the meek; he hath sent me to bind up the broken-hearted, to comfort all that mourn; to appoint unto them that mourn in Zion, to give unto them *beauty for ashes.*" You will remember that this scripture Jesus read in the synagogue of Nazareth and applied to Himself. Let us for a moment withdraw from a world in ashes, and from the exciting prospect of its renovation, to find those particular cases of misery to which the words were originally addressed, to comfort them that mourn in Zion. If we may venture to ascribe to Christ, what is commonly observable in men, some master quality of mind that gives its nature to all the rest and manifests the individuality of the person, that quality in our blessed Lord is tenderness. For Him the house of mourning had a peculiar charm; it was there His brow was lightened by those gleams of joy that sometimes irradiated for a moment the habitual sadness of the Man of Sorrows. He was in His element when tears were to be wiped away and burdens were to be lifted from the oppressed, when sins were to be forgiven and sobbing hearts quieted; and even when He feasted and rejoiced with His people, the occasion was the festive thanksgiving of recent mourners; every guest there wore a garment of praise for some special tenderness shown him in extremity. My dear brethren, let me preach *Jesus, the same yesterday, and to-day, and for ever.* Where are they who, like Job, are sitting in the ashes of loneliness and sorrow ? Do you mourn under the Lord's displeasure? Are you tasting the bitterness of unpardoned sin? Unto you is the word of this salvation sent. Hear and receive the blessing pronounced upon them that mourn;—*O thou afflicted, tossed with tempest, and not comforted; behold, I will lay thy stones with fair colors, and lay thy foundations with sapphires.* Have you been so long in sackcloth, that you begin to fear that the mercy of God is " clean gone for ever ?" So might have thought the poor woman whom Satan had bound for eighteen years; and the Bethesda patient, who for thirty and eight years had lain upon the edge of the water of life, but could never get in : but beauty was reserved for both; the evermindful Friend came by; and there could be no *inveteracy* when Jesus touched the disease. O, doubt it not, that this Saviour is present *now* to raise you from the dust. *Believest thou that I am able to do this for thee?* Answer Him at once; and if the affirmative is embarrassed by a misgiving, break out in the desperate confidence of one in a similar distress, "Lord I believe, help thou my unbelief!" No, sorrowing friend, thou shalt not be sent away without comfort. Whatever the cause of thy mourning, if it afflicts thee, it grieves Him. Bare thy heart to this incomparable physician: bid Him touch the secret sore, bid Him probe it: believe in His skill, in His love, in His heart. No mother ever touched her ailing child with so cautious and watchful a ministry as He will address to thee: He will pour into the wounds of thy spirit the balm of His forgiving love, and bind them up, and invest you with the beauty and salvation of His righteousness.

APPENDIX.

NOTE TO PAGE 141.

IT hardly suits with the candour and honest thoroughness which are said, by the disciples of it, to be the distinguishing merit of a certain Theological School, to throw, as writers of this class commonly do, a haze, half philosophical and half poetical, around the doctrine of the CROSS. The death of Jesus Christ as the consummation of a *pattern*, and the same event considered as an *appeasing offering*, are two ideas so plainly marked off from each other, that no man need teach his brother the difference between them. It is true that if we take the pains to analyze them, we may find a ground common to them both, where they run into each other and become the same thing. The good man *is as* the wicked man *ought to be;* and the latter, in deriving benefit from his example, may be saved from punishment in one of these two ways;—the example may atone for him, and in this sense be the price of his escape; or its virtuous efficacy may deter him from further sin, and be the means of his reformation; in either instance there is a vicarious element. But is it fair to attempt to get rid of the directly sacrificial nature of the death of Christ, unmistakeably defined and clearly affirmed because intended for the apprehension of common people, by ignoring in it the circumstance of *penal substitution?* If Jesus did not die in our stead, that is, in the sacrificial sense, to appease wrath and to purchase acceptance, a sense sufficiently intelligible in all languages, it is better to say so clearly and decidedly, instead of investing a plain idea in philosophical mist! But the truth is, that the New Testament so positively and variously declares that the blood of Christ was a "ransom," and that we are " bought with a price;" and its doctrinal and practical writings are so unanswerably based upon this view of the Saviour's crucifixion, that it requires considerable learning and more ingenuity to make people believe anything else concerning it. The most painful symptom of unbelief in the present day is this *handling of the word of God deceitfully,* this blowing from the Gospel trumpet an uncertain sound. Let the writers against whom we make this complaint, return to the compositions of Paul, and answer this question, not to their consciences, but to their honest critical judgment. Could any writer understanding the sufferings and death of Christ as *they* expound them, have written of the CROSS as the Apostle has done in his Roman and Corinthian Epistles?

LONDON:
PRINTED BY HAYMAN BROTHERS,
GOUGH SQUARE, E.C.

www.ingramcontent.com/pod-product-compliance
Lightning Source LLC
Chambersburg PA
CBHW030817230426
43667CB00008B/1253